Unscripted

Cheryl Hines

Skyhorse Publishing

Copyright © 2025 by Cheryl Hines

All Rights Reserved. No part of this book may be reproduced in any manner without the express written consent of the publisher, except in the case of brief excerpts in critical reviews or articles. All inquiries should be addressed to Skyhorse Publishing, 307 West 36th Street, 11th Floor, New York, NY 10018.

Skyhorse Publishing books may be purchased in bulk at special discounts for sales promotion, corporate gifts, fund-raising, or educational purposes. Special editions can also be created to specifications. For details, contact the Special Sales Department, Skyhorse Publishing, 307 West 36th Street, 11th Floor, New York, NY 10018 or info@skyhorsepublishing.com.

Skyhorse® and Skyhorse Publishing® are registered trademarks of Skyhorse Publishing, Inc.®, a Delaware corporation.

Visit our website at www.skyhorsepublishing.com.

Please follow our publisher Tony Lyons on Instagram @tonylyonsisuncertain.

10 9 8 7 6 5 4 3 2 1

Library of Congress Cataloging-in-Publication Data is available on file.

Hardcover ISBN: 978-1-5107-8373-7
eBook ISBN: 978-1-944824-36-5

Cover design by Brian Peterson
Cover image by Daniel Prakopcyk

Printed in the United States of America

*Dedicated to my nephew Michael.
He was the essence of joy.*

Note to Readers

Please keep in mind as you read this book that the events and experiences detailed here have been faithfully rendered, as I remember them, to the best of my ability. Some names and identifying details of the people and places involved have been changed for privacy reasons.

I've retold conversations as I recall them, and they are not meant to represent word-for-word documentation.

Thank you to all the people who show up in my memoir. You've been part of my journey through life, and I love you, or at the very least, like you a lot.

I couldn't have written this book without my sister, Becky. We had some late nights, long talks, delirious laughs, sentimental tears, and philosophical takes on the meaning of life.

Thank you to my husband, Bobby, and my kids, Catherine, Bobby III, Kick, Conor, Kyra, Finn, and Aidan for loving me.

Chapter 1

One phone call from Larry David in the fall of 1999 changed the trajectory of my life. I didn't know it at the moment, but that fateful call would set my life on a path that would color my world for the next two decades and beyond.

"Hey, HBO wants to turn the special into a series, and I would like for you to play my wife," he said.

"Oh my god. That's the best news I've ever heard!" I said.

"I hope that's not true. Please tell me that's not true." he replied.

"It *is* true. This is a dream come true for me," I said.

"Don't say that. There has to be other things that have happened that are better than this."

"No, actually, this *IS* the best news I've ever heard."

"Okay, Okay. Well, somebody from HBO should be calling you soon."

"That's great. That's really, really great. Thank you so much!"

"Okay, all right. I'll talk to you later."

Cheryl Hines

The project he was referring to was a one-hour comedy mockumentary for HBO in which Larry David returned to the world of stand-up comedy following his years writing and producing the iconic TV sitcom, *Seinfeld*. That special was the genesis for the long-running series, *Curb Your Enthusiasm*.

I was thirty-four years old at the time. That's geriatric for a young woman trying to break into the entertainment industry. I had been in LA since my mid-twenties trying to get my foot in the door, and fortunately for me, they were looking for an unknown actress with strong improvisational skills. Up until then, my biggest acting role had been an episode of a TV show called, *Swamp Thing*, and quite frankly, my dramatic death scene had not sparked the notoriety I had naively anticipated. Although I had spent many years in college studying theater and television production, it wasn't until a serendipitous encounter with a legendary comedic actor's sister that I discovered the world of improv.

I'd been bartending at the InterContinental Hotel since my arrival in LA. One night an affable woman took a seat at the bar. She unraveled a map of the city and asked me to point out Melrose Ave.

"Can you help me find the Groundlings Theater?" she asked.

"Okay, let's see. . . . Why are you looking for it?" I asked.

"My brother got his start there, and I want to go see a show while I'm in town."

I had never heard of The Groundlings Theater.

"They have the best comedy shows," she explained.

"That sounds fun. Who's your brother?" I asked.

"Phil Hartman. He was performing there when he was discovered for SNL," she said casually.

"You're kidding! Phil Hartman! I love him."

"Oh, you know who he is?"

"Oh my god, Phil Hartman? He's the best. I watch him every week. How did he get from the Groundlings to SNL?"

"They have scouts that come and watch the shows, looking for new cast members. They saw him perform and sent him to New York to audition," she said.

I couldn't believe what I was hearing. I had just discovered the path from LA to SNL! *And* I had met Phil Hartman's sister!

My next night off from work, I beelined for the Groundlings. I was beyond impressed by what I saw on that stage. I watched the funniest, smartest, silliest people I had ever seen perform sketch and improv in that little ninety-nine-seat theater. It was like a portal into another world I desperately needed to be a part of. I didn't know it at the time, but the Groundlings launched many comedic powerhouses; Laraine Newman, Cheri Oteri, Kristen Wiig, Chris Parnell, Melissa McCarthy, Maya Rudolph—the list goes on.

I quickly learned the only way to ever have a *chance* of performing there was to take classes and work through the different levels of their school for the unlikely chance that someday, you might be invited into the company. There was only one obstacle: I had no money. I was so broke, I didn't even own a refrigerator.

When I returned to work at Angel's Flight (that was the name of the InterContinental's bar) I talked incessantly about the Groundlings. How amazing the actors in the show were. How that night had inspired me. How I knew my life would change if only I could take the first Basic Improv class. I talked about it *so* much that for my birthday, the regulars and the waitstaff chipped in to pay for my first class. It remains the best birthday present I've ever received.

My teacher was Lisa Kudrow. I counted the hours between classes. I couldn't wait to see her, watch her, and learn everything I could possibly learn about improv. Although she's only two years older than I, she seemed so much more worldly. I was twenty-seven when I started classes there.

I bartended, waitressed, and worked as an assistant's assistant for the next seven years, trying to make ends meet while I made my way through the levels of the Groundlings program. After many, many improv and sketch-writing classes, I was invited to perform in the Sunday Company—the level just before an aspiring comedian was either cut from the program altogether or invited into the main company. Due to the reputation of the theater, industry insiders would often frequent the theater to look for new talent. I was finally able to garner the attention of an agent. But even with an agent, I struggled to land an acting job.

One night I was performing in a sketch show, and unbeknownst to me, Bob Weide, who was slated to direct Larry's special, was in the audience. I had written a sketch about an earthquake safety consultant visiting an LA office to review its earthquake safety procedures.

My character, an office supervisor, was feeling insecure because she didn't know any answers to his questions and was being shown up by her fellow workers who seemed to know everything about earthquakes.

"Do you light a candle after an earthquake?" he asked.

"No, because there might be a gas leak," one of my work mates replied immediately.

"Great job! You're right! And where do you go if you feel the earth starting to shake?" the consultant asked.

"Crawl under a table for cover," someone volunteered. "Or stand in a doorframe!"

"Excellent! You're right," the consultant applauded.

My character was feeling a mushrooming anger as she fell behind in the competition. She was determined to answer the next question and beat her coworkers to the punch.

"What do you do if your water supply is cut off?" he asked.

"Well, if push comes to shove," I blurted out confidently, "you can drink your own urine."

My answer earned me an awkward silence and uncomfortable glares from my coworkers, not to mention an arched eyebrow from the fire official. After an agonizing pause, he broke the silence with a more delicate suggestion.

"Orrrr . . . you can drink the water that's still in the hot water tank," the consultant said.

The faux pas sent my character into a spiral.

"I don't drink my own urine if that's what you're thinking," I felt prompted to explain. "I never will. I don't care how bad the earthquake is, you couldn't make me drink it."

"Nobody thinks you do," the consultant said testily.

He tried to move on to the next question, but I interrupted.

"It's not like I come home from work and drink a nice tall glass of my own urine," I told the room reassuringly.

The earthquake safety official tried to move on again, and again I interrupted.

"I thought we were talking about an apocalyptic earthquake where there's nothing left. No hot water tanks or anything. And you know what? Even if there *was* an apocalypse and I was surrounded by zombies, and the only way I could survive would be to drink my own urine, I still wouldn't do it."

"We get it," said one of my coworkers.

"I said, 'if push comes to shove!'" I screamed.

This went on and on until I asked a coworker to pass me my coffee mug and she was scared to touch it.

That was the sketch.

The next day I was called in to audition per Bob's recommendation. I had no idea what I was auditioning for, only that it was a new project by Larry David, the co-creator of *Seinfeld*. I had never met Larry or Bob before. I was told in advance there was no script, and the show would be improvised. As the casting director, Marla Garlin, escorted me down the long hallway to the audition, she kindly informed me that the show was supposed to feel like a documentary, and if at any point it felt fake or false, the audition would be over. She also said that my character had been married to Larry for a while and didn't put up with his bullshit. Just before she opened the door, she said,

"Oh, and don't touch Larry. He doesn't really like people touching him."

"Okay," I said.

I walked into a small room filled with producers, including Larry and Jeff Garlin.

"Oh, Urine Girl!" Bob greeted me.

"Thank you for that title, and I hope that doesn't stick," I said.

He went on to tell them about the urine sketch. Urine Girl turned out to be a moniker that *would* stick with Bob. It proved to be quite the ice breaker.

Larry turned to me and said, "Okay, let's imagine we have kids and I don't eat chicken anymore. That's all you need to know. And we'll just improvise."

"Okay, great," I said.

So, Larry and I started talking. He asked me what was for dinner.

"Green beans, potatoes, and chicken cacciatore," I replied.

"Why would you make chicken cacciatore? I told you I'm not eating chicken anymore." He asked, exasperated.

"That's okay, you don't have to eat it. The kids and I still eat chicken—you can just eat more of the beans and potatoes," I said.

"Why would you even make chicken if I told you I'm not eating chicken?" he pressed me indignantly.

"Well, because WE still eat chicken," I said.

We went back and forth for a while and then the audition was over. That was it. We said our goodbyes, and I left. As I was walking down the hall toward the elevator and the droll routine of my life, Marla caught up with me.

"Can you go in and do one more scene with Larry?"

"Of course."

I went back in.

"Can I talk to you about something?" Larry asked sternly, "I don't think you put enough milk in the kids' cereal bowl."

"Well, I cover the flakes," I said.

"Okay, well, let's just fill it up to the top of the bowl," he said.

"That's a waste of milk," I said. "They're not going to drink it. I just cover the flakes, and then they can have a glass of milk if they want."

"We can afford it. Let's just fill it up to the top of the bowl," he said.

This exchange went on for a while with me refusing to budge. Everyone seemed to enjoy it. I had somehow tapped into the tone they were looking for.

I got back in my unair-conditioned Toyota Tercel and continued to run errands for my boss. A few hours later, my agent called to tell me I got the part. In an actor's world of callbacks and network testing, it was a lightning response.

"Wow. That's great. Could this turn into something else? Like an ongoing show?" I asked my agent hopefully.

"No, this is just a one hour special," he replied. "It'll probably just be a few days of work. But congratulations. You did it!"

I wasn't going to make much money, and I definitely wasn't going to be able to quit my day job, but I still felt like I had won the lottery. I was going to get to work with Larry David. *The* Larry David.

Chapter 2

The only things that were important to me when I was growing up were family and becoming an actress. I was twelve years old when Jimmy Carter became president. He had a thick Southern accent, and I initially thought it was great because he sounded like my parents.

My mom and dad were both born and raised in Florida and had never ventured out of the state except for one long year when they moved us to Albany, Georgia. My dad had landed a good job as a regional manager for Burger King. My mom was from Jacksonville, and my dad was from the tiny town of Frostproof. While politics was never discussed in my house, I once asked my mom who she voted for, and she replied, "that's nobody's business."

I couldn't help but notice how President Carter was taunted on TV for his Southern drawl. It was the first time I realized some people equate the provincial accent with slow-wittedness. I decided that wasn't going to be me. I wasn't going to be a hillbilly. I was going to do whatever it would take to be a successful actress, including losing my vernacular.

Growing up in Winter Haven, FL, I walked to Sunday mass each weekend with my mother, my brothers, and my sister. Our church was right across the street from our house. It seemed important to my mother, so we'd dress up and go and try to stay awake for an hour while a priest read from the Bible in an Irish brogue and spoke of love, forgiveness, and the other virtues. When he mentioned tithing, I bristled at his request for ten percent of our income; my parents were barely scraping by. Sometimes my mother, then working as a teaching assistant, would take a second job to make ends meet.

After church, the priest would come over to watch football with my dad. They had a blast sitting in their recliners, drinking beer, and yelling at the TV when a player would fumble or miss a touchdown pass. My dad's version of time with the priest seemed so much more gratifying than my mom's. I don't recall my dad ever actually walking into the church, but he had a "Honk If You Love Jesus" bumper sticker on his El Camino.

Dad was a little rough around the edges and loved to cuss and curse. When he was driving, he'd call people names for no reason whatsoever. Someone would drive by and honk, as his bumper sticker suggested, and he'd smile and wave and say, only loudly enough for whomever might be in the car with him to hear, "Alright, dumbass. Keep moving."

My dad was a good ole Central Florida country boy. Tall, handsome, and lanky, he had been his high school football hero and prom king. He had a warm and charming personality, a raucous laugh, and was a great dancer. His favorite diversion was shooting avocados out of the tree with his pistol.

Dad was charismatic and smart, but he lacked the attention and perseverance of a successful businessman. One day in 1978, he pulled up to the house in a stripped-down cargo van and announced that he had quit his job and bought a fleet of mopeds. And by fleet, I mean three. We were living in Tallahassee at the time, a town that had two major universities, Florida State University and Florida A&M University, and he was struck with the notion that a business renting—or selling—mopeds to students was a sure thing. How could they resist the opportunity to zip around campus on a motorized two-wheeler? The miracle machine, half bike, half scooter, with a capped speed of 35 mph, was becoming very popular elsewhere, and he wanted to get in on the ground floor and build his moped empire. He was always having lightning strikes of this sort of inspiration, and there was a very small space between his impulses and action. Unfortunately, his projects were often way before their time, and his execution frequently lacked consideration of key details.

Was the plan for him to sell the three mopeds and then buy more as needed? How would he market the idea to students without signage or advertising? The answers to such questions were never properly resolved.

I was in middle school at the time, so I didn't pay much attention to the nuts and bolts of the business plan or its implementation. Not sure there *was* a business plan. Unfortunately, the moped empire was never realized.

While the mopeds broke down or simply disappeared, we got to keep the van. When she was sixteen, my sister Becky gladly drove the cargo van. My friends and I were thrilled that we had a way to get around. There were a few caveats though. Money was always scarce and so, predictably, was gasoline. There was never enough gas to get us through the week, so we got used to the routine of pulling over when the tank was empty and then leaving the van on the side of the road. It was understood that we'd have to either walk the rest of the way or call a willing parent to pick us up wherever we ran out, which we did every week around the day before Becky's next paycheck.

Also, there were no seats in the van, besides the driver's seat. We sat cross-legged on the carpetless floor and tumbled into each other at every turn. Someone finally found a chair for the passenger side, but it was a rolling office chair that added one more challenge to the carpool. One lucky person would get to sit in the chair as it rolled quickly and violently around the back while the others had to dodge and weave to avoid getting their fingers run over or getting pinned in the corner by the flying chair. Ah, those were the days.

I recall Frostproof as a magical paradise of endless orange groves with an aroma of citrus hanging in the thick, sticky Florida air. We spent most weekends with my dad's mother Ruth. She was perfect. She worked as a bookkeeper until she was ninety years old. She would take us to work, equipping us with paper and pencils. While she sat at her adding machine, we four kids played "office" for hours. Somehow that's all we needed. She gave us all a good foundation in work ethic and an appreciation for family that has survived for generations.

Grandma's shortcoming was cooking. She hadn't the patience. Her bacon was limp and transparent. "No thanks," we would tell her politely, "That chunky oatmeal really did the trick."

Grandma once told me, "When I got married, I told your grandfather I didn't know how to cook, so he'd never ask me to. It worked. He always did the cooking!"

Her advice often pertained to marriage strategies: "A good man is hard to find," she told me, "But a bad one is even harder to get rid of."

My grandmother was right about a lot of things. Except bacon.

For a time, my grandparents lived in a trailer next to the orange grove that my grandfather managed. When we were little, my grandaddy Earl would put us kids in the back of his pickup truck and take us through the grove to help him with the irrigation system that pumped water from his pond into long pipes among the orange trees. Armed with metal coat hangers, he deployed us to poke through the sprinkler holes clogged by minnows from the pond. We'd do this for hours in the blazing Florida sun. Somehow, it remains among the most fun jobs I've had. Or maybe just the most memorable.

When we were finished, Grandaddy would pile us in the back of the truck and drive back to the trailer, through the grove. When the sprinklers turned on, he'd turn his truck off and then act like he couldn't get it started. We'd get drenched sitting there in the flatbed, screaming and howling at him through the back window to let him know we were getting soaked. We could see he had pulled his hearing aid out of his ear. It dangled from the battery in his front shirt pocket. Earl knew comedy and specialized in sight gags.

At night we'd sit happily in that steamy trailer and have TV dinners. My grandmother would always say, "I wonder what the poor people are doing tonight?" acting as if we were in a big suite at the Plaza Hotel.

My grandfather died young of lung cancer. He started smoking at a time when people didn't fully realize how harmful cigarettes were. I could hear his agonizing coughing fits through the flimsy trailer walls. My grandmother told me, "One of the hardest things to do is to quit smoking. You should just never start." I always took her advice. I never took up smoking. Even when I was in the film *Waitress* and my character smoked, I was reluctant to practice. My daughter, Cat, was only three years old at the time and I couldn't bring myself to smoke around her, so I waited until we were actually shooting the scenes to try to master the technique. To this day my sister makes fun of the awkward way I held my cigarettes in the movie.

***

Carol Burnett was my North Star. Becky and I would sneak out of bed to watch *The Carol Burnett Show*. We weren't able to laugh for fear of being discovered on the other side of the half wall that divided the TV room from the dining room, but hearing my parents laugh was like a shot of serotonin. Every show sent me on a magic carpet ride. I'd forget about having to stand in the "free lunch" line at school. I'd forget about my panic when the timer went off before I could finish a test. I'd forget about the names other kids would call me because of my unusually large teeth. The skits were pure joy.

The cast, Harvey Korman, Tim Conway, and Vicki Lawrence were brilliant, silly and smart. I didn't get the context of some sketches, like when Carol was doing a spoof of *Gone with the Wind* and walked down the stairs wearing the dress she made out of the curtains—complete with the curtain rod across her shoulders, but even at my young age, I knew it was hilarious. Her timing, the costumes, the musical numbers all testified to her comedic genius.

That show inspired Becky and me to write and perform our own "hilarious" sketch shows. Whenever my parents had company, we'd put a show together for the grown-ups. We recruited our brothers, Chris and Mike, as begrudging cast members. The adults would sit on the ends of our beds, and we performers would use the closet as a backstage holding area. It was a tight squeeze in that closet when you had three or four kids in there waiting to "go on."

These performances continued for years until our TV broke. Without Carol for inspiration, we were rudderless. The television was a heavy console with a record player on one side, a TV in the middle, and a radio on the other side. Since we couldn't afford to have it fixed, music became my new obsession. In 1974, when all of our friends were watching *Happy Days* and *Sanford and Son*, we were listening to the radio all day and all night. We knew every word to every song like "I Am Woman," "Ballroom Blitz," and "Billy Don't Be a Hero." Becky, Chris, Mike, and I would act out the story of Billy, volunteering for battle and losing his life. It was a dramatic musical turn for The Hines Players, but it was a crowd-pleaser nonetheless.

In those formative years, I couldn't have dreamed that I'd ever get to meet Carol Burnett, but indeed I did. One of my best friends from the Groundlings, Julie Welch, had grown up with Carol and invited her to one of our shows. Imagine! Carol Burnett watching me perform sketch comedy. The stars in the universe had aligned.

***

I looked for every opportunity at high school to hone my acting skills. Unfortunately, Leon High's drama department offered slim pickings. Mr. Hoyt was tone deaf to Tallahassee's cultural rhythms. Despite Florida's sweltering heat, our groundbreaking rendition of the 1557 Elizabethan "comedy" *Gammer Gurton's Needle*, encountered a chilly reception. Unimpressed by our rhyming couplets, even the parents revolted. At our closing night performance, Mr. Hoyt was alone in the audience. At least we got a standing ovation.

It was Leon's chorus department, led by the dynamic Mr. Hightower, that had the community clamoring for tickets to see shows like *Call Me Madam* and *The Sound of Music*. So, I leaned in.

It's fair to say, I wasn't Mr. Hightower's favorite. It was not just my enthusiasm nor my subpar singing that annoyed him. His principal gripe was that everything made me laugh. He was an overwrought and earnest musical conductor, and the spectacle of this intense impresario directing a high school chorus seemed to me inherently hilarious. When a singer missed a note or sang off key, he would stomp his foot, clap his hands, and angrily point at the offender. There was more drama every day in that chorus room than there was in our entire run of *Gammer Gurton's Needle*.

"You're never going to get anywhere because you don't take life seriously enough," he told me.

That was hard to hear from someone I revered. Nevertheless, I also found it terribly funny. My laughter sent him into a tailspin. At his instruction, I put a rubber band on my wrist. "When you feel the urge to laugh, snap the rubber band as hard as you can. The pain will override your impulse, and you won't find things quite so funny," he said sternly.

It had the opposite effect. A few days later, an apoplectic Mr. Hightower was berating a boy who was out of rhythm.

"You're a beat off, Dan! A *beat off*!" he screamed.

The adolescent giggling that followed the double entendre transformed into a cacophony of hysterics when my fellow chorus members noticed me frantically snapping the rubber band against my wrist. That was the end of any cordiality between Mr. Hightower and me. The boisterous laughter didn't die down until he shouted,

"Take it off! Just take the damned thing off!"

I locked eyes with Hightower and slowly, dramatically slid the rubber band off my wrist. To keep from laughing, I bit the inside of my cheek so hard it drew blood. It worked! But I had made an implacable enemy of someone, who at the time, I felt held the keys to my future.

Things really came to a head during my senior year. Again, I auditioned for the big chorus show, and again, Mr. Hightower sidelined me as a chorus girl. Mano a mano, I sat down with Mr. Hightower to tell him I didn't want to be a chorus girl again, but I'd do anything else for the show: lighting, costumes, sound, production.

"Then you will NOT be a part of the show at all. You will NOT be allowed to go on the chorus trip to New York, and the Madrigals (an a cappella group I was also in) will NOT sing at your mother's wedding as previously planned."

Those vindictive bullets lodged straight into my heart. Despite the pain and shock, I refused to give him the satisfaction of seeing me cry. I struggled to understand his strong punishment. The prospect of losing my theater engagement sent me into a deep depression. Finally, I turned to someone I truly trusted to help me make sense of it all, my psychology teacher, Dr. Linda Rogers. I told her everything. She asked if I'd go with her to talk to the principal and explain what had happened.

Oh God, the principal's office! Please God, not the principal's office!

The next day Mr. Hightower didn't come to school. A student passed me a note during one of my classes:

Do not discuss family matters with other people. Please come to my house after school. Mr. H.

It got worse by the second. Was this it? Was I going to get whacked after school? I did as he said. I didn't tell anyone about the note or that I was going over to his place to talk to him. I arrived to find him sitting on his front porch in a rocking chair. I took a seat next to him. His demeanor was unusually calm.

"I've spoken with the principal," he said coldly. "You *will* be allowed to go to New York. You will *not* be allowed to work on the show in any way whatsoever, and the Madrigals will *not* sing at your mother's wedding."

That was that. I learned a lot from Mr. Hightower. Hard lines, discipline, and resilience. It's all served me well in my life's journey.

I got to fly for the first time when we went to New York and when my mother's wedding rolled around, fifteen classmates showed up to sing an eight-part, a cappella version of "When I Fall in Love." In compliance with Mr. Hightower's directive, they weren't there as the Madrigals, they were there as my friends.

***

I paid little attention to anything in school that didn't have to do with theater or chorus. That included my classes. I despised both gym clothes and PE, so I found a loophole: Becky told me I could get PE credit for going to softball practice. She was an athletic superstar, playing shortstop for the varsity team. She was tough and talented in sports, and I was just the opposite. When we were growing up and played football in the backyard, Chris would quarterback and say, "Mike, go short and turn around. Becky, you go long and turn around and Cheryl . . . you just run around."

I joined the varsity team when I was a freshman, knowing full well I would never have to play. It worked out perfectly too because one of the girls on our team had a baby whom she needed someone to hold during the games. I gladly sat on the bench, held the infant girl, and cheered on the team with all kinds of songs, chatters, and chants. I had been kicked off of the cheerleading squad due to bad "citizenship" grades because I talked too much in class, so I had plenty of cheerleading experience. My friends would wave to me in their polyester PE uniforms as they begrudgingly ran laps around the track. They were jealous, and with my encouragement, *they* decided to sign up for softball the next year. I envisioned a relaxing season, sitting on the bench, surrounded by my grateful friends sharing my babysitting duties and following my cheerleading directives.

My scheme backfired. The flood of unexpected new recruits prompted the school to launch a JV team, and we all actually had to play. To make matters worse, I was assigned shortstop because I had already "played" varsity. It's not an exaggeration to say we were the worst team in the region. My best friend Linda would sit on her glove while playing centerfield, and my other best friend Valerie would kneel down and plead for the coach to take her out after every pitch she threw. And when the ball came to me, I'd run away from it as fast as I could. Our only saving grace was a ten-run rule—when a team was ahead by ten runs, they'd call the game. That's how every game ended—zero to ten. Despite it all, we had more team spirit than any team in the panhandle. We didn't let the scoreboard ruin our good time.

We all lettered in softball. Thank you, Lady Lions.

Not all the teachers at Leon had it in for me. Coach McHenry, the basketball coach who also taught biology, seemed to "get me." When presented with a dead frog, belly up, pinned to a board, I balked.

"I'm not cutting this frog open," I told him.

"Well, you can't get a grade higher than a C. This is what we're doing all semester," he said as the class looked on.

I glared at the scalpel and that poor little guy crucified to the corkboard. "Okay, coach, I'll take the C."

"Well, what're you going to do while everyone else is doing their assignment?" he asked.

"I don't know. Hang out with you, and you can tell me what I'm supposed to be learning," I said.

"You better move your desk close to mine then. I'm not going out of my way to make an entirely different curriculum for you," he relented. I dragged my desk across the room.

Biology became my favorite class. Coach McHenry and I would joke and chat during class while the rest of the students donned safety goggles to perform amphibian autopsies. "If you want to try to raise your grade, I can give you an extra credit assignment," he whispered to me.

"I'm listening."

"I'll give you extra points for every basketball game you go to. The football program gets all the attention here. We need some bodies in the bleachers. Bring your friends," he said.

Now he was playing to my strengths. My softball career had honed my aptitude for cheerleading. I showed up for every game with my crew in tow. I'd stand up and wave furiously to make sure Coach McHenry knew I was there. He'd see me and wave me off as he huddled with the players on the court. When report cards came out, I was shocked to find I still got a C in biology.

"Hey, why did I get a C? I went to every game," I said.

"Yeah, well, it raised your grade. You didn't do anything all semester. You would've gotten a D. But you learned a lot about basketball, right?" he asked with a smile.

"Coach!" I exploded.

"Ok, ok. Let's talk about it. Tell me what else you learned in this class and let's see if you can convince me to change it," he said dryly. He eventually changed it to a B-. In later years, Coach McHenry would call me every so often and say, "Hey, I think I'm watching you on TV. Are you on something called *Match Game?*" he asked.

"Yep, that's me," I replied.

"Ok, I thought so. I guess I'll keep watching it then. Way to go, Hines," he said proudly.

I really loved that guy.

As graduation neared, my friends were picking their college destinations as I opted for beauty school. I knew I'd need a way to make a living while I pursued my acting career, and it only took a year to get a cosmetology license.

At the age of seventeen, I was the youngest in the class. Ms. Gowdy did her best to teach me how to cut, color, perm, and Jheri curl. I quickly learned the art of a "pocket perm" after unwittingly overprocessing a patron's hair. Sometimes an entire rod would break off and plink into the sink while shampooing the perm solution out. I'd discreetly fish it out and put it in my pocket so the woman never had to see the chunk of hair that she had lost. Let's be honest, anyone who came to Lively Vo Tech to get a $5 perm knew they were rolling dice. Our classroom always smelled of harsh chemicals and burnt hair.

Ms. Gowdy referred to us as her babies even though our class consisted mostly of middle-aged women. She was wise beyond the world of beauty and a bit of a stoic.

"You know, babies, sometimes life doesn't work out the way you want it to, and you have to get a bottle of wine and sit on the beach by yourself until you sort it out."

I found myself on the beach quite often with a Bartles & James wine cooler in hand, wondering if my life was on the right track.

My newfound skills proved to be a hit at keg parties. Broke college students would line up for haircuts. The more beer I drank, the more creative I got. "That's what I like to call a bi-level mullet with a twist," I'd say as I hurried someone out of my chair. "Next!"

It seemed like everyone I knew was in college except me. My high school sweetheart, Lee, had moved back to Morgantown, West Virginia, to go to WVU. I managed to scrape enough money together from my night job as a waitress to visit him. I met all of his friends, and we went to a football game and party after party. I had a blast. While I was in Morgantown, I even got to meet his dad, a successful businessman. I sat with him one day in his impressive office.

"Why aren't you in school, Cheryl?" he asked.

"I am. I'm in cosmetology school," I replied.

"You don't want to go to college? Get a degree? Maybe in theater?" he asked.

Up until that point, nobody had asked me that.

"I can't afford it," I said matter of factly.

"You know there's student aid and grants you can apply for to help you. I think it's something you should consider. You don't want to look back and regret that you didn't have a college experience."

He was right, I didn't. There had to be a way to go to school with no money. After all, Chris and Becky were going to Florida State University and they didn't have money.

"Why don't you go visit the theater department there? They have an excellent theater school. I'll make a call and have someone show you around tomorrow," he said.

Make a call? Who was this man and who was he calling? How did I get dropped into this world of a parent sitting down with me, in his office, talking about my future? I was intrigued and inspired.

***

I finished cosmetology school, cut hair during the day, and waitressed at a nightclub called Studebaker's so I could save money for WVU. Located just down the road from the state Capitol, every night we'd be packed full of politicians and businesspeople. I worked my way up to become a bartender. My first night behind the bar, the other bartenders presented me with a shot glass filled with a murky brown liquid.

"What is this?" I asked.

"It's a Matador."

"I've never heard of it before," I mildly protested.

"Well, you need to know what it is. Everyone has to drink one on their first night. It's part of your initiation." I downed the putrid potion.

"What the hell is in that thing?" I choked.

"We drained the bar mat."

It was a sickening way to learn a useful trick. Once in a while, a poor, desperate college student would approach the bar and sheepishly ask me for a Matador. It was a creative way to get a free drink.

"Sure," I'd say knowingly as I'd pick up the mat I'd been pouring drinks on and fill up a shot glass with the collected liquor, juice, cream, and debris. Having a glamorous name for the dregs somehow made it less humiliating.

My younger brother, Mike, worked with me as a deejay. He and another deejay would pack the dance floor as they lip-synced to songs from the fifties and sixties. When they'd play the Isley Brothers' *Shout*, all of the employees would have to jump on the bar and dance. Everyone in the club, every last legislator, would shimmy and strut and sing at the top of their lungs. When his partner quit, I leapt at the opportunity to join my brother Mike in the deejay booth.

"We just don't have female deejays," my manager, Jimmy, told me.

"Maybe it's time you do," I said. I was confident in my vast knowledge of music, even from that genre. All those years I spent during our broken TV era huddling around the console listening to the radio, playing records, and dancing with my dad left me with an encyclopedic knowledge of fifties, sixties, and seventies tunes. Becky and I knew what songs got him going. Dad couldn't resist hitting that shag carpet when we'd play James Brown and Chuck Berry. We always took delight in his dancing. He would strut and shuffle around the living room for hours. Man, did he have some moves.

"Give me a trial run," I said to the Studebaker's manager. "If it doesn't work out, I'll stay behind the bar."

"Deal," he said, as he gave me a big bear hug.

It wasn't long before Mike and I became the Saturday night, must-see deejay team. We were so popular that a local radio station would broadcast our show live. Our mom and stepfather, Dan, would burst with pride every week as they tuned in and partied by the pool with their friends in their little beach town close by. Mike and I would make her feel like a celebrity when we'd say, "This one goes out to Shell Point. Hi Mom!"

***

I saved up money, moved to West Virginia, reunited with Lee, and launched my college career. Before the year was up, in short order, I'd broken up with Lee, run out of money, and returned to Tallahassee.

I started taking classes at Florida State but hadn't fully settled in when my brother Chris, recently graduated, lured me to

Orlando. He kept sending me newspaper articles announcing that Universal Studios was building a new movie facility in the city and telling me I *had* to be a part of "Hollywood East." I decided I could get a degree from UCF instead of FSU, so I moved to Orlando and lived with Chris until I could get on my feet. My older brother was always looking out for me.

"Hey, what's wrong with your ears?" he asked me one morning soon after my arrival.

"My ears? Nothing, why?" I responded.

"I keep finding Q-tips covered in black stuff," he said.

"Oh, I use those to take off my mascara," I assured him.

"Oh, okay. I didn't know anybody did that. I was thinking, what the hell is wrong with her?" he said, relieved I didn't have gangrene of the inner ear. "And is this yours?" he asked as he held up a small tool, rubbing the edges of it trying to make out what its use could possibly be.

"Yes, I use that to scrape off the calluses on my feet," I said.

After that he didn't touch my stuff and dismissed any other mysterious objects as things I needed for my "lady problems."

Chris was the conservative one in the family, and when I got a second job as a chatline monitor, I had a hard time convincing him I wasn't a phone sex operator even though my chat name *was* Cookie. I worked for 1-900-999-CHAT. For 99¢ a minute, you could call and talk for hours to a friendly group of strangers and me. My job was to keep the conversation going, make sure nobody was rude or mean, and more importantly, to stop anyone from having phone sex. We were a respectable chat line. No matter how many times I told them not to, a few callers would insist on trying. I shared a cubicle with the Horoscope Hotline and the Joke Hotline. Whenever I had a couple on a private chat and I knew they were ramping up for some sexy talk, I'd put them on speaker to entertain the other monitors, Destiny and Squiggy, before I'd cut them off. One night, I had some mavericks on the line. Things started out as usual: "What do you do for a living?" the girl asked.

"I'm a doctor," he said unconvincingly. "What do you do?"

"I'm a supermodel," she said seductively. "What are you wearing right now?"

"Um, a suit. What are you wearing?"

"Nothing except high heels. How big are you?" she asked.

"What?"

"You know. How *big* are you?" she repeated.

"Oh, I'd say about four inches," he replied.

Destiny couldn't help herself. She broke in and said, "Hello? You're on the phone, you can at least lie about it!"

One time, Squiggy called in sick, and I had to man the Joke Line. For just 99¢ a minute, you could call in and hear one joke after another. With my book of jokes in hand, I answered the phone to find a guy at a fraternity party on the line.

"What the hell is this?" he asked.

"You've called 900-999-JOKE," I said. "What did the grape say when the elephant sat on it?"

"What?"

"Nothing, it just let out a little whine."

"Are you kidding me? That's the worst joke I've ever heard," he said. Then he called out to some guys, "This chick just told the dumbest joke."

He passed the phone to another guy. "Who is this?"

"My name is Cookie."

"Is this a phone sex line or something?"

"No, it's a joke line. Why don't cannibals eat clowns?"

"What is this?"

"Because they taste funny."

"What are you doing? I don't understand what's going on," he said.

"You guys called the joke line so I'm telling you some jokes," I said. "What do you call a fake noodle?"

"What?"

"An impasta."

"Do you think that's funny?" he asked me.

"Here's another one if you didn't like that one. What do you call a bear with no teeth? A gummy bear."

"This girl is a lunatic," he said to his friends.

He handed the phone to another guy. "What kind of shit are you trying to pull? Why did you call here?"

"You guys called me. Hey, why did the scarecrow win an award?" I asked.

"I don't know, why?"

"Because he was outstanding in his field."

"This is bullshit," he yelled.

The more jokes I told, the angrier they got but they never wanted to hang up.

"Hey Cookie, what do you look like?"

"Don't worry about it," I said. "But why did the math book look so sad?" I asked.

"No, I'm being serious for a second."

"Because it had too many problems." I said.

"Cookie! Why are you doing us this way? Come on!" the fraternity guy pleaded.

I made a lot of money for the Joke line that night and I amused myself for hours.

***

The Universal Studios theme park was getting set for opening day. As the empty production soundstages prepared to welcome the crowds, I stood in line to audition with a thousand other wannabe actors. We wore numbers pinned to our shirts like Marathon runners. After countless call backs, I was ecstatic when they chose me to perform. It was a live show that celebrated Alfred Hitchcock's films. I was finally a professional actress. Dressed only in a flesh-colored bodysuit and a wig, I played Janet Leigh and recreated the *Psycho* shower scene in front of thousands of tourists. A volunteer from the audience would pretend to stab me with a rubber knife as I screamed bloody murder in the shower. It wasn't what Chris had envisioned for me in Hollywood East, but I loved the job.

Finally, a TV show started shooting at Universal: *Swamp Thing*, based on the film of the same name. I auditioned twice to no avail. A few months later, I got called in for a third audition but didn't get the part. However, they offered me a nonspeaking role in which I would emerge from a swamp, topless. I couldn't help but tell my fellow *Psycho* actors about my chance to be a Swamp Goddess. My accommodating friend, Mark, beckoned me into the bathroom of our trailer for a private chat.

"Hey, if you're thinking about not taking this part because you're concerned about your breasts, I'm willing to take a look at them and give you my professional opinion," he said.

"Oh wow. You'd do that for me?" I asked.

"Yeah, yeah. I would. Nothing weird, you know. Just actor to actor," he reassured.

I crossed my arms and grabbed the bottom of my shirt. I started to lift it and reconsidered.

"Just actor to actor, right?" I asked.

"Yes, yes. Professionals," he said. Again, I grabbed the bottom of my shirt, started lifting it, and reconsidered.

"I'm not sure if I want to be known as a swamp goddess, you know?" I asked.

"Well, let me just see and we can talk it through," he said impatiently. Again, I started lifting. Again, I reconsidered.

"I mean how would I even put that on my resume? It's basically a featured extra," I said.

Mark looked at me deadpanned. "You're not going to show them to me, are you?" he asked.

"No."

"You never were, were you?"

"No."

These were the games we played in our trailer between shows. My sense of decorum overrode my ambition, and I passed on the bit part, but my failure to land a job pulled me into a well of self-doubt. Only my sister could help me at a time like this.

"I don't know what to do. I can't even get a role on *Swamp Thing*. *Swamp Thing*! It's the only show shooting here and I can't book a part. I've auditioned three times! Maybe I'm just not a good actor. Maybe it's a sign that I shouldn't be doing this. Becky, *Swamp Thing* doesn't even want me," I said.

"I think you're right, Cher. You should get out of this business," she said calmly.

"What?"

"Yeah, you've picked the wrong profession," she said.

I was shocked to hear those words coming from her mouth

"Do you know how much rejection you're headed for? It's almost always going to be rejection. Once in a while you'll get something, but if you're distraught over *Swamp Thing*, I don't think you're going to make it. You're just going to be depressed all the time. It's not worth it," she said. "Life is too short."

I perseverated over that for quite a while. She was right. I had to toughen up. I was too sensitive. I cried too much when I was a kid: when I saw a roach, or if my hospital corners weren't perfect when I made my bed, or if my potatoes touched my broccoli. When I got a bad grade on a paper, which for me was anything less than an A, I buried the paper in the neighbor's back yard. This was particularly absurd because my parents never even looked at my papers or grades. Also, since I was little and dug a really shallow hole, the neighbors ended up finding the papers, and I looked like a lunatic.

The thing that *really* set me off was when the timer dinged before I finished timed tests in math. Hearing "pencils down" sent me into hysterics. My third grade teacher took me out of class and sat with me on the sidewalk.

"What do you think all the crying is about?" she asked.

It seemed pretty obvious to me, but I answered anyway.

"The way you scream PENCILS DOWN," I replied. "I know all of the answers, but you don't give me time to finish."

"I know you do. You're one of my best students."

Finally, we're getting somewhere.

"Have you ever noticed the other kids don't cry?" She asked.

"They all finish in time," I said.

"Not always, you'd be surprised," she said. "What happens if you get a bad grade? Do your parents get mad at you?"

"My parents? No. They never ask about my grades," I said.

"Maybe you should think about saving your tears for really important things."

"Like what?"

"Are your grandparents still alive?"

"No, my grandfather just died a little while ago."

"That's a good time for tears. You lost your grandfather. That's important. It doesn't matter if you don't finish your test or if you don't get an A."

I stared at her long and hard. It doesn't matter if I don't get an A? What????

"The next time you hear me say, pencils down, take a deep breath and tell yourself it's okay. Because it IS okay. No matter what grade you get, it's going to be okay," she said as she touched my arm.

She was so sure about what she was saying, I had to believe her. From that day on, I saved my tears for things that mattered. It took every fiber of my being—it simply wasn't in my nature. Thus began the lesson of letting go.

Once again, I had to let go a little. I had to look at rejection as a stepping stone that would lead me to the next opportunity. I needed to embrace failure as part of the journey. I made the decision to consider every audition as the final destination, an achievement in itself. Looking at it this way, no amount of rejection would frighten me. It was a paradigm shift. Maybe I had untapped resilience.

Becky knew what she was doing all along.

***

I got a fourth audition for *Swamp Things*, and landed the biggest role of all, a mad-scientist-seductress who had killed someone and was trying to steal a top-secret formula. Lines such as "it's not like I don't know a thing or two about molecular cold fusion" rolled off my tongue before I was about to kill again! The only way to stop me was . . . the beeping of a faulty smoke alarm.

"What exactly am I dying from?" I asked the director.

"You know, when you pulled the plug on your stepfather's life support machine, you heard the beeping of his heart monitor. Now the beeping from the smoke alarm is haunting you and drives you crazy," he explained.

"Right, right. Like 'The Tell Tale Heart,' I get all that, but how do I die?" I asked.

"Look, we don't have a lot of time here. Drop the gun, clutch your heart and fall," he said hurriedly.

"Like a heart attack or something?" I asked, for clarity.

"Yeah, okay. A heart attack, but just do it fast," he said as he walked off to take his seat behind the camera.

After we wrapped, I was pretty confident my performance in *Swamp Thing* would be my ticket to stardom. I'd accomplished all I could in Orlando and was ready for LA. I gave my two weeks' notice at Universal, sold my worldly possessions at a garage sale, and packed up my Toyota Tercel.

Before I could leave though, an unexpected call came from my stepfather, Dan. It didn't sound like his normal, joyful voice. He wasn't doing one of his comedy bits like answering the phone, "Hello, Sherwood Forest. Robin Hood speaking." Instead, he was quiet and somber.

"Hey, I just want you to know, I've been diagnosed with liver cancer. Your mom is in denial. I just love you so much and thought you should know," he said softly.

My heartbreak changed everything. I immediately drove to Tallahassee to visit him in the hospital.

"He's just having a little episode, but he's looking pretty good," my mom said cheerfully.

He *wasn't* looking good. His skin was an odd shade of yellow.

"Rosemary, can you go try to find me a ginger ale somewhere?" he asked.

As the door closed behind her, Dan motioned for me to come closer.

"Can you do me a favor? Call hospice. Here's the number. I'd really like to go back to Shell Point. Sorry to put this on you but it would mean the world to me."

"You got it."

I called the number.

"Hi. My stepfather is in the hospital and asked me to call. I'm not really sure why. What exactly is hospice?" I asked.

"Well, usually if it looks like someone is near the end of their life, we can arrange for them to go home and give them the care they need," she said delicately.

"Oh, I don't think that's the case here. What do you consider near the end of their life?" I asked.

"Of course, there's no hard and fast rule and we are always hoping for recovery, but usually if a patient has been diagnosed with three months or less, we're able to help," she said. "Do you want to share your stepfather's number? I can get some more information and call you back."

It seemed like no time at all before she called me back.

"So, we would be able to help Dan go back home," she told me.

"Really?" I asked incredulously. "If this were to happen, when would he make the move?"

"He wants to go right away. We can have a hospital bed delivered tomorrow."

We moved Dan back to their house. Becky and I stayed with my mom and Dan and tried to be as helpful as possible. We'd keep Dan company while my mom went to work and kept him as comfortable as possible. He rarely asked for anything, but one night he wanted frozen yogurt. I called to see what flavors they had.

"Mango and vanilla," the young guy said.

"Okay, great. What time do you close?" I asked.

"We close at nine," he said.

Dan told us he'd love mango, so off we went. We were worried we might not make it there before they closed, but Becky drove like a bat out of hell. Dan never asked for anything, and we were determined to get that friggin' yogurt. We got there just in time.

"We'll take a quart of mango, please."

"Oh, our machine isn't working today," he said.

"What? Didn't I just talk to you on the phone? I asked what flavors you have," I said testily.

"Yeah, those *are* the flavors, but our machine is down," he said casually.

When we returned empty-handed, we told Dan what had happened, and he laughed so hard it sent him into coughing fits.

"He told you the flavors but didn't think to tell you the machine was broken!" he howled.

He kept his sense of humor through it all.

It was only a few weeks later he took his last breath in the living room as Jimmy Buffet played softly in the background. He was surrounded by Chris, Becky, Mike, me, a few of his closest friends, and my inconsolable mother.

The thought of moving across the country and leaving my mom in her fragile state was unimaginable. Universal kept me on as I made the five-hour commute from Orlando every few days to check on her. When I returned to the *Psycho* trailer, my friends steered clear of me. I asked Mark why.

"No one knows what to say. We don't want to make you sad," he said. "No one can bear the thought of making you cry."

He pulled me close and held me for a long time. All my friends lined up, and one by one, they hugged me and cried with me. I had saved up a lot of tears.

Six months later, my mom told me it was time for me to go.

"I'm going to be alright," she said. "I promise. And nothing would make Dan happier than for you to go to Los Angeles and pursue your dream. It's time."

Chapter 3

I only knew a few people in LA, and one was Becky's high school boyfriend, Paul. He had a bit of a Tennessee Williams's Brick in *Cat on a Hot Tin Roof* quality, minus the angst and with a lot more humor. Indisputably handsome, 6'3", perfect brown hair, green eyes, a muscular swimmer's build, and a lightning wit, and rapier tongue. He was theatrical and always delivered non-stop laughs. His feigned indignation, and humor always shed light on some annoying hypocrisy or awkward truth. We loved him.

My strongest high school memory of Paul is him effortlessly dragging me across the stage in a musical number from *Call Me Madam* as I clutched to his leg wearing a 1950s satin dress. He sang and danced with ease, ignoring me as I desperately clung to him in my role as a socialite "hanger-on." The number brought down the Leon High auditorium. Looking up at him that night, I could have never known the path our lives would take.

After high school, Becky was still close to Paul, and they talked regularly as he made his way from Tallahassee to LA, stopping a few years in New York City, where he found himself. I hadn't seen

Paul in a few years when I set out for Hollywood, and I couldn't wait to see his beautiful face. Promising Becky he'd take good care of me, he and his boyfriend, Eddie, anxiously awaited my arrival.

The drive from Florida to LA turned out to be less relaxing than I expected, mainly because I had agreed to bring a guy I had just broken up with along for the ride. Nearly every state provided me with new reasons to recall my grandmother's warning about certain men being hard to get rid of. I relented to his request after he agreed that we would "just go as friends." I ended up calling him Cool Jazz because that's all he wanted to listen to. Whoever was driving would get to control the radio, so I did most of the driving.

Furthermore, I was really emotional about leaving home. My siblings were supportive but sad that I was leaving. They also knew it was even more sad for me, so rather than long good-byes, they wrote me notes to read along the way. It was going to take several days to get to LA, and they told me to open a letter a day. With my sisters-in-law also writing notes, I had just enough to get me through the trip. The notes ranged from sweet, "Whenever I see something beautiful, it will remind me of you," to funny, "I expect you to be prancing around Santa Monica in your thong, fulfilling the dream you've had for so long." I really looked forward to reading them at the end of a grueling twelve- or fourteen-hour drive. That was the best part of the road trip.

LA was a culture shock for us both. As we made our way through Beverly Hills, staring at the gorgeous Mercedes, BMWs, and Rolls Royces, we got nervous when a cop pulled up behind us. We were convinced there had to be some sort of city ordinance against operating a dilapidated Tercel with a weird luggage pod on it, so we made an unplanned turn and lost him.

When we got to Paul's, Eddie was standing on the street between two cars, saving a parking space. Naturally, that was something Paul would have delegated. I immediately fell in love with Eddie. He was also funny and handsome but quieter and more sensitive than Paul. The Boys, as I'd come to call them, gave us a grand tour. We saw the stars on Hollywood Boulevard, the Santa Monica Pier, the Griffith Observatory, the Hollywood sign, and The Comedy Store on Sunset Boulevard.

"Okay, I think you've seen everything, now you're probably ready to get back home," Paul said to Cool Jazz. Cool Jazz was on the next flight back to Orlando.

Paul worked as an extra in movies and TV. He *loved* it. He was a regular stand-in for Ted Danson on *Cheers*, made appearances on sitcoms like *Murphy Brown*, and was even a butt double for the actor Alan Thicke in Fruit-of-the-Loom underwear commercials. The Boys traveled on a shoestring budget in between jobs. There was something admirable about Paul's utter lack of material ambition. He found happiness in each moment. I, meanwhile, was chasing the dream, and I was broke. The reality of actually trying to survive in Hollywood really hit me.

With the help of an old friend from *Psycho*, I got a bartending job at the InterContinental Hotel downtown and settled into a small one-bedroom, rent-controlled apartment. It didn't take long before I had my first authentic LA experience. After working the closing shift, I got home at around 2:30 a.m., and I was really hungry. The only food I had at my place was ice cream. I thought, *Well, I shouldn't eat ice cream at three in the morning, but, ah, fuck it. Life is short.* So I ate a lot of ice cream and fell asleep.

The next thing I knew, I was startled awake because the earth started shaking. I could see my blinds swinging and I thought, *This can't be a hurricane, I'm in LA.* I looked outside. It was pitch dark and every car alarm on the block was going off. I thought, *Oh my God, we've just been bombed. I'm gonna die.* My next thought was, *I'd be so mad at myself right now if I die and my last thought is—I should've eaten that ice cream.*

It was 1994, before cell phones, the electricity was out, and I wasn't sure what was happening. My brother, Chris, called me on my landline and said, "I can't believe your phone works."

"I know, it's crazy. I don't know what's going on over here," I said.

"You guys just had a huge earthquake," he told me.

"Oh my God. How do you know?" I asked.

"I'm watching the news. It's 7:30 here. What are you doing?" he asked.

"I don't know. I don't know what I'm supposed to do."

"Well, stay on the phone with me," he said, and began talking me through my next moves. "Go open your door and see what people are doing. Try to figure out if you're supposed to evacuate."

I opened my door. "No one is in the hallway. I don't see anyone running outside or anything." I reported this to Chris.

"Okay," he said, "make sure there's no broken glass anywhere. You don't want to cut your feet. If people aren't evacuating, stay inside. Things could be falling, you know, power lines, so maybe it's better to just stay put."

And then my phone went dead. The service dropped. Paul and Eddie walked all the way over from their apartment to check on me. For some reason, they brought me socks.

"Yeah, somebody was selling socks on the corner, so we thought, okay, maybe there's some reason we need to bring you socks," Paul said.

The Boys were always taking care of me. They were the cornerstone of my early LA life. They encouraged me to try everything, to talk to anyone and go anywhere. And over the years, we did! Once my career started, they were my dates to the Oscars, to the Emmys, on ski trips, to parties, to plays and musicals and stand-up shows. We always had a great time together. They were the perfect date—Paul with his classic good looks and Eddie with his rock-star edge. Eddie was around six feet tall and had shoulder-length, dark brown hair and blue eyes. He was thin and fit. He was always handsome in the off-beat clothes he found at thrift stores, woven leather or cloth bracelets, and casually brushed back his hair. If we were going to a fancy party, Paul would wear a traditional suit while Eddie would wear a blue velvet suit with a stripe down the side of the pants. We were always the first on the dance floor, and I'd have to beg them to leave to avoid being the last ones at the party. They made everything fun.

The three of us were inseparable during the eight years before I got *Curb Your Enthusiasm*, and they became my protective shield as I was getting more and more recognizable. I would walk in everywhere, arm in arm with those two, the buffers, my tall and beautiful dates running interference. Paul loved all of the glam and wanted to meet every celebrity. If Sharon Stone was at the party, he wouldn't have asked me first if I wanted to meet her. *He* wanted to meet her, "Oh, Sharon, Cheryl Hines wanted to meet you. And I'm Paul Beckett, and this is Eddie."

Before I met my first husband, Paul Young, I had convinced myself I'd never get married. Miraculously, The Boys helped me get into an apartment right below theirs. We were practically living together and saw ourselves going through life as a unit. Paul was the organized, dominant personality, Eddie was the sensitive soul of our group, and I was the driven one, always leading us to our next glamorous adventure. Even in the early days, albeit an untraditional path, we were sure we three would be together forever.

Years later, when I was married to Paul Young, The Boys would happily take me to events when my husband wasn't available. One day, he came home while The Boys and I were getting ready for a premiere. My husband looked at Paul Beckett and said, "Is that my new shirt?"

"Of course," I said, "He needed a nice shirt."

"Why do you have to wear my new one?" Paul Young asked.

"It was the nicest one in there," Paul Beckett said.

"It's a big premiere, Paul. He needs to look good. Don't make this awkward," I said.

Paul Young was always outnumbered. "Okay, you guys have a good time."

***

Paul and Eddie liked to show my visiting friends and relatives around town. Paul was a tour guide in Los Angeles for a while, so he was very knowledgeable about the city's history. It was perfect because they had endless energy and no jobs. They could be in charge of what someone else "had to" experience.

My mom loved Paul and Eddie, too. She had known Paul since he was part of our friend group in high school. The Boys always took good care of her when I had to work. They would pick her up from the airport and bring her to my apartment. Most of the time they would just fold her into their daily routine. Sometimes they'd take her to the gym or sit with her outside a café and drink coffee for hours.

They were a funny trio. When Paul proposed going to the French movie *Indochine*, she said in her slow Southern drawl,

"Now, I don't know French and I don't like subtitles, so I don't think I'm going to enjoy this movie."

"Rosemary," Paul said, "This will be good for you. How much do you know about the latter years of the French colonial era in Vietnam?"

"Well, I don't know anything about it," my mom said.

"Great. We're all gonna learn about it tonight. You can go back to Tallahassee and tell everyone you watched the new Catherine Deneuve film," he said.

"Now Paul, I'm never gonna remember that name and none of my friends in Tallahassee will care if I watch a foreign film or not," she said.

"We're gonna watch it and you're gonna love it," Paul said sternly.

About fifteen minutes into the two and a half hour French film, my mom was sound asleep. Every so often Paul would nudge her and say,

"Rosemary, you're gonna miss the good part."

One day, Paul and Eddie took my mom to Best Buy so she could surprise me with a new TV. Then they surprised her with a trip to the West Hollywood Pride Parade. My mom had never seen so many scantily clad, good-looking guys in one place before. She couldn't quite understand why *she* was there. When I got home from work there was a lot of excitement between the TV purchase and hearing my mom's description of their adventures at the Pride parade. I really got an earful. Mainly, my mom had a lot of questions: "Now, why were there so many naked people in the parade and is that legal?"

She went to a Catholic school as a girl, and her mother taught her how to be a proper lady. She taught The Boys and me how to enter a room. "When you walk into a party, you should stop at the door or the entryway before you go inside. Let it frame you and then drop your coat down so everyone can see your outfit and take you in. Then you can walk into the party."

The Boys and I entertained each other endlessly with this party tip. Anytime we would go anywhere, even Starbucks, we would stop in the doorway, drop our jacket down and pose so people could take us in. No one ever "took us in." We'd smile and nod as if the whole room was watching.

My mom's name is Rosemary, but most of my friends and family call her Cracklin Rosie—Cracklin' for short. When she became a grandmother to my niece, Kailey, and my nephew, Graham (Mike's kids), my mother didn't want to be called grandma, so my sister and I appropriated the nickname from Neil Diamond's hit song.

Quick side note. I was fortunate enough to be cast in *Keeping Up with the Steins* and Neil Diamond sang at a bar mitzvah in the film. I brought a picture of him with me to get his signature for my mom. Before he walked onto the set, we were advised not to bother Mr. Diamond, not to talk to him or make eye contact with him. So I kept his photo in its envelope, tucked into the side pocket of my set chair.

As the day went on, Neil came up and started talking to me. I wasn't sure what to do. I'm a rule follower by nature, and I was panicked that someone was going to see me talking to him and think I was violating the directive not to bother him.

"Can I be honest with you?" I asked.

"Please do," Neil said.

"I'm having a great time talking to you, but we were all told to leave you alone and not bother you," I said.

"What? Oh, no. Yeah, I think they do that sometimes. I don't know why," he replied.

"I'm not even supposed to make eye contact with you," I told him.

He laughed, "Oh, no! Come on!"

Then I told him about my mom and her nickname and the photo I had with me.

"Will you please go get that photo right now so I can sign it to your mom?" he asked.

"Oh my gosh, yes. Thank you so much!" I said.

I retrieved the photo, and he signed it to my mom:

Rosemary, thank you for keeping Cracklin' Rosie alive in your grandchildren's hearts.

Love, Neil Diamond

My mom just loved it. She hung it in her living room to make her friends jealous.

***

I managed to live below The Boys for about five years, before the rent became too much for me. I moved in with my friends, Maria and Mandy, who were migrating to LA from Orlando.

I knew Mandy from back home. Maria recalls me asking her to lunch to interview her for approval. In truth, I just wanted to see if we would vibe together. I really liked having roommates from Florida. They reminded me of home. I was working a lot of late hours, but we still found time to spend at the Snake Pit, a dive bar on Melrose. On hot days, we'd sit in front of the apartment building in a kiddie pool, drink beer and watch our neighbors parade past. West Hollywood was full of actors, musicians, writers, and various flamboyant characters. Los Angeles is home to the most creative people on the planet, and individualism is an artform in West Hollywood. It was always entertaining.

Paul Beckett lived by the principle, "If everyone's laughing and only one person is crying, go for the joke." When you were that one person, it could be infuriating. One thing everyone knew about my roommate Mandy—especially Paul—was that she could *not* keep a secret.

Mandy came up to me one day and said, "I can't stop thinking about that really embarrassing thing that happened to you, but Paul Beckett told me to never bring it up to you because it will only make you mad."

"Just tell me what he told you because I don't know what you're talking about," I said.

"Well, he told me about the story when everybody threw a surprise party for you. You came home and didn't know anyone was there because everyone was hiding. Before anyone yelled *surprise*, you went straight to the cupboard and got some peanut butter. You lifted up your skirt, put peanut butter on your vagina, and called the dog over to lick it off.... Then you realized people were watching..."

"Mandy, Paul Beckett told you that?" I asked.

"Yes, and he told me you would get mad if I brought it up," she said.

"Yes, I'd get mad because that's not a true story," I said.

"This is exactly what he told me you'd say," she said.

Finally, I said, "Mandy, first of all, I've been living with you for the last three years. I don't have a dog. Why weren't you there? Nothing about this story makes sense if you think about it."

"See? Paul was right. You are getting mad," she said.

"Mandy, first of all, what kind of friends do I have that don't jump out and yell *surprise* when I walk in, but instead, watch me open the cupboard, get the peanut butter out, and hike up my skirt? I don't have one friend that would say, 'Hey, Cheryl, there are people watching. Whatever you're about to do, don't do it.'" I said, "This never happened. This is an urban tale that's been whispered down the lane. Paul planted this story with you because he knew you'd tell people."

Even though I laid out the implausibility of the story, I could not get her to believe it never happened. I was living with her at the time of the supposed event, but even that didn't seem to move the needle. I tried my best to convince her it wasn't true.

The worst part was, she sat on this story for probably two years. I'm sure she told many people about the dog and peanut butter and said, "Whatever you do, never bring this up with Cheryl."

When I confronted Paul Beckett about it, he laughed and said, "Cheryl, didn't you tell me that happened?"

"Of course not! And by the way, why weren't you at the party? No one you know was at my surprise party. Who were the people there?" He just laughed and said, "Cheryl, I knew you'd be mad."

That's just who Paul Beckett was. If one person cries and everyone else laughs, the joke is worth it.

Chapter 4

I worked at the hotel for six years. *Six years!* I learned every part of the job and became a Renaissance woman. In a pinch, I could fill in for waitresses, hostesses, cocktail servers, or deliver room service dinners.

Part of my job was putting big wooden panels over the liquor when I locked up at night. The only way to do that was to jump up on the bar and secure the panels. Problem was, all the women who worked there were required to wear skirts as part of their uniform, and I was the only female bartender.

I told my manager I couldn't possibly wear a skirt because of the bar-jumping duties and asked if I could wear pants. He told me that it was impossible because they didn't even *have* women's pants at the hotel. We had a long conversation, and I stood firm that it was imperative for me to wear pants. Finally, he relented, "I see. Yes, that makes sense. I suppose you could go buy some women's black pants and we can reimburse you."

When I went to work for the first time wearing my pants, I felt like Sarah Connor from *Terminator* walking into the hotel in slow motion. Other employees stopped in their tracks to stare at me. I felt like a badass rabble-rouser.

I loved the people I worked with and even played on the softball team. As I've already established, I'm not a good softball player but this beer league was well within my skill set.

The league had a no-slide rule, which didn't hinder me since there was no way I was going to slide no matter what the stakes were. One night I was rounding third, coming into home, when I tripped and fell face-first into home plate. The umpire said, "You're out for sliding!" My whole team came off the bench to defend me.

"She would never slide! She fell!"

"Well, I don't know," he said. "It looked like a slide to me . . ."

The other team flooded the field. "That was a slide! You can't slide!" they yelled.

Everyone was yelling.

"Did you slide or did you fall?" the umpire asks me.

"Are you kidding me? Do you think I'd slide face first? I fell."

"All right, safe!" he yelled and gestured theatrically. The other team was furious.

After the game, we all went out for beer and talked it through until both teams were on speaking terms again.

***

I had a lot of good times with my InterContinental friends as the years passed while I attended auditions and waited for my "big break." Then one night at the Angel's Flight, Phil Hartman's sister put me on my trajectory to the Groundlings Theater. Driving home from that first night in the theater, I remembered something that happened before I left Florida. I was in bed, eyes closed but not yet asleep. Suddenly, I felt a strange *presence* next to me. I very distinctly, very clearly heard a man's voice whisper in my left ear: "You know the joke."

At the time I remember thinking, *Does that mean I should lean into comedy?* That first Groundlings show answered the question. My plan had just become very clear.

From that moment on, I just wanted to be around those magical people. I thought, if I could somehow be a part of that theater, I would be able to learn everything I needed to about comedy. The next day, I called to inquire how to get my foot in the door. They explained the system to me. You have to start in a beginner's improv class and work your way through the school. Actors are cut along the way, and only a few are invited into the company. I immediately signed up for an audition. Afterwards, I was told I was eligible to take the class.

There was only one problem: I didn't have any money. At that point in time, I was barely making ends meet.

I could think of nothing but the Groundlings. I woke up thinking about the Groundlings. The Groundlings was the last thing I thought about before I drifted off to sleep. Apparently, I talked about the Groundlings incessantly as well—to anyone who would listen.

The bar was full of different characters. A manager of one of the big baseball teams stayed at the hotel and visited me every night. He only talked about baseball. Always baseball. Only baseball.

"Don't you ever get tired of talking about baseball?" I finally asked him.

"Don't you ever get tired talking about the theater?" he shot back.

That made us both laugh. He was telling me about strike outs, and I realized I was only telling him about punchlines. I went on and on to my fellow waitstaff and my bar regulars about the show I saw at the Groundlings and how much I desperately wanted to take a class there. As I mentioned earlier, to my surprise, for my birthday, they all chipped in to buy me a spot in my first class. In retrospect, they probably realized it was the only way they could get me to shut up. I couldn't believe it. My heart was filled with love and gratitude. It was the best birthday present I had ever gotten.

Years later, when we were shooting the first season of *Curb*, I was filming a scene at a bowling alley with Larry, Ted Danson, and Mary Steenburgen. I heard somebody yell, "Cheryl!"

I looked over and saw my friends from the hotel bowling a few lanes over.

"What are you doing?" my friend yelled from his lane.

"We're bowling," I said. "I'm actually shooting a show."

They all cheered. I smiled, waved, and gave them the "shhh" motion to remind them we were filming. I hope they know that their gift literally changed the course of my life.

***

Having Lisa Kudrow as my first improv teacher was more than I would've dared to dream. At the time, she wasn't on *Friends* yet, but I knew her as a recurring character on the show *Mad About You*. I couldn't wait to go to class every week. All I ever wanted to do was go to that class, listen to Lisa, and watch Groundlings shows. She was funny, gifted, and incredibly intelligent.

Since I couldn't afford to buy a ticket to all of the shows, I asked someone in the office if I could volunteer in exchange for being able to stand in the back. I would collect tickets as the audience filed into the theater, then I'd stand in the back and watch Will Ferrell, Cheri Oteri, and Chris Parnell perform. It was heaven.

I continued taking classes, watching shows, and working at the InterContinental when, in January 1995, the O. J. Simpson trial began. The jurors ended up sequestered at my hotel, which was just five blocks from the courthouse. Judge Lance Ito didn't want their location disclosed, so we weren't allowed to tell anybody they were there. The entire fifth floor was dedicated to the jurors, and no one was allowed to go there without authorization.

Every day was filled with gossip about the trial and the jurors. Eight and a half months of solitude made those sequestered jurors stir-crazy. They weren't even allowed to watch television. I could step out onto the plaza just outside of the Angel's Flight lounge and see that one of them had etched "Help me" in their window.

At the outset of the trial, we were all on high alert. My manager told me to pack a suitcase and leave it by my door so I could rush to the hotel as soon as deliberations ended.

The Rodney King riots were still fresh on people's minds, and no one knew what would happen in the streets of LA when the verdict was read. My manager wanted me to check into the hotel so I could stay there and cover shifts in case chaos erupted downtown and other employees weren't able to get to the hotel. On October 2nd, after just four hours of deliberation, the jury reached a verdict. My manager called, sounding oddly calm and serious, "Cheryl, it's time. They're going to read the verdict tomorrow. Leave *now*," he said as if I were a CIA operative.

I jumped into my Tercel, sped downtown, and checked myself in. I felt so important. It was the first time in my life I would ever stay at a five-star hotel. When my Dad came to visit, he described it as "So goddamn expensive it costs you $5 to fart and another five to smell it."

My room was gorgeous, and I was told to order from room service when the employee cafeteria wasn't available. Let's just say, the employee cafeteria never seemed to be available.

For the next few days, I'd greet a coworker at my door, wearing my plush bathrobe, as they wheeled my breakfast into my hotel room. We would laugh while we'd set up the little room service table together.

Ultimately, O. J. was acquitted of both murder charges. I didn't get to spend much time in my beautiful room because the hotel was very busy, and I had to cover a lot of shifts.

So, that is my O. J. Simpson story. Twenty-nine years later, during my husband Bobby's presidential campaign, *Newsweek* ran an article at a time when the media was looking for any excuse to attach our family to a scandal. There was a picture of O. J. Simpson and a picture of me, side-by-side. The headline was, "Cheryl Hines Reveals Connection to O. J. Simpson." It seemed like a stretch considering I never met him, Judge Ito, or any of the jurors, but, a headline is a headline.

***

It was also at that bar where I met a young investment banker visiting from New York named Charlie. He was handsome and funny. He would sit at the bar, have a drink, and we would talk for hours and hours. He asked me out on a date.

"I'd love to, but my mom is visiting, and I can't leave her by herself in my apartment," I said.

"That's OK. Bring her with you," he responded.

So the three of us went to dinner and I was enamored. He had to leave town the next day, but we talked on the phone every night. The next time I saw him (I guess you could call it our second date) was when we went to Maui together. He paid for my flight, and I got us a free room at the InterContinental in Maui. Everyone thought we were on our honeymoon, so we just went along with it. I fell madly in love with Charlie. He was everything I wasn't. He had a real career with responsibilities. He knew what he was doing in life. Sometimes we'd argue over the value of money. He was quite driven by it and he felt I didn't care enough about it. Making money and having money were his defining metrics of value. Every time we drove by a Starbucks and people were sitting around drinking coffee in the middle of the day he'd say, "Doesn't anybody in this town have a job?"

It always made me laugh because I knew he was serious.

It was during this time I wrote, produced, and starred in a play on Theater Row.

The mere thought of performing in a theatrical run without getting paid seemed crazy to him.

"I'm not like you. You could be happy living in a trailer. I want more for myself," he'd say.

Although I had no aspirations of living in a trailer, he was right, I could be happy living in a trailer. That concept alone was enough to spark long discussions about the meaning of happiness and the value of money.

Despite our differences, we clicked on a lot of levels and really had fun with each other. Eventually, he moved to Los Angeles. We didn't move in together, but we had keys to each other's apartments. We traveled to exciting places like London and Portugal. He was the one with the money and I was the one with the hotel hookup. We dated for a few years, and even though our lives were so dissimilar—he with his investment banking friends and me with my artsy, funny, broke friends—we really had something special. Between Charlie bankrolling it, a generous Angel's Flight regular chipping in, and me using my credit card with the ridiculously high interest rate, I was able to produce a full theatrical run.

Charlie, Paul, and Eddie were in the front row of every performance.

One Sunday morning, I drove to Charlie's apartment and turned the key. When I walked in, I knew something had happened the night before. I quickly realized he had cheated on me. I was devastated. I gathered all of my things, threw them in the car, and left. I told him I never wanted to see him again. I was so heartbroken I couldn't sleep. The only way I allowed myself to sleep was to set an alarm so every hour I'd wake up and cry until I was dehydrated, and then I'd set another alarm, drink some water, and go back to sleep. My heartbreak was so agonizing that sometimes I felt I couldn't breathe.

My InterContinental friends could see my utter despair. I had befriended a hotel security guard named Joe who would always walk me to my car at 3 a.m. to make sure I got there safely. Joe was a giant of a man, standing around 6'7" and weighing 375 pounds, but he had a kind heart. Joe could tell something was wrong. With some prompting, I gave him the details of my breakup with Charlie.

"I can't stand to hear that," he said. "I know a guy who could take him out," he offered. "He usually charges 10K, but if I ask him to do it as a favor, I know he would."

"What? What are you talking about? You wanna have Charlie killed?" I asked incredulously.

"I'd do that for you," he answered.

"That's very sweet of you to offer, Joe, but I don't want Charlie *killed*."

"That guy deserves it," he said.

"Joe! No!" I protested. "You absolutely cannot do that!"

"Okay. What's his last name and where does he work?" he asked in a professional voice.

"Why?" I asked.

"I'll just wait for him to get off work, and when he's walking to his car, I'll take out his knee with a crowbar. I'll just do it myself. We don't need to get anyone else involved if that'll make you feel more comfortable," he told me.

If that would make me feel more comfortable?

"Oh my God, no. Please don't. I'll never tell you his full name or where he works." I told him firmly, adding gently, "but I really appreciate the thought."

I knew this was Joe's love language. I couldn't imagine anything more awful than having Charlie come out of work and see Joe coming at him with a crowbar!

"Cheryl, you deserve better," he said sweetly.

He was right. I assured him that I would never allow Cheating Charlie to hurt me again. We wouldn't require any physical action. Joe finally accepted my demurral.

"Well, I'm here if you ever need me."

"Thank you, Joe. That means a lot." I said sweetly.

My hands were shaking as I got in my car and gripped the steering wheel. It was a long ride back to my apartment. My head was spinning with thoughts of murder and Cheating Charlie and crowbars and Joe and underground hitmen. I knew I wasn't in Tallahassee anymore. Anyhow, you're welcome, Cheating Charlie!

***

It was soon after the Cheating Charlie incident I turned thirty. I was still a bartender and didn't have an agent. There were no signs of a hopeful future. I was hitting a new low.

At least with Charlie, it seemed like my life had meaning. He was spellbinding, and when we were together, I felt like everything was moving forward. For the first time, I had considered a relationship just as important as being an actress. I was completely committed to Charlie, even if it meant I might end up in the suburbs one day, an idea that was previously inconceivable. I thought he loved me, felt the same way I did, so his actions came as a shock. I was left feeling small and foolish.

He called me for weeks and months after, but I never picked up. One day after work, I walked out, and he was there waiting for me. I was surprised he knew I was working that day because I was filling in for someone and it wasn't my usual nightshift. He insisted I listen to what he had to say. He apologized and told me he was starting to panic at the idea of getting married. *Why was he panicking about getting married?* I wasn't even positive I ever wanted to get married, and I had never brought it up. But he said he was feeling pressure from family members, friends, and even himself. He even confided in me that one of his female coworkers, a woman I had met many times, warned him that I was probably trying to trap him. After all, I was a lowly bartender with no future, so if I got pregnant, he would be forced to marry me and I'd be set with a wealthy, handsome husband.

Standing in the hot sun, still sweaty from working the lunch crowd, those words struck me. Is that how people saw me? I glanced around and saw other women dressed in expensive suits, hurrying to their offices. I looked down at my ugly, worn, black rubber-soled work shoes. Of course that's how people saw me. I had a pit in my stomach thinking about the conversations he must've had with his coworker. I couldn't take another minute of the humiliating conversation. "I never thought I'd say this to you, but I have to say goodbye."

I knew it would be the last time we would hug each other, and I wished my hair didn't smell like kitchen grease, but it did. After a long embrace, I broke away from Charlie and walked to my Tercel without looking back. It felt like something inside of me had died.

Self-doubt began to creep into other areas of my life. *Why am I so far from home? Where is my life going?*

Recalling my beauty school teacher, Ms. Gowdy, I'd sometimes grab a bottle of wine, sit by myself and try to sort it all out. Forsaking the beach, I'd go up to Mulholland Drive, perch on the side of the mountain and stare down at the twinkling lights of LA and wonder why I let myself get so far away from my family.

I desperately missed them. Fortunately, my two best friends, Paul and Eddie, were my LA family. They always looked out for me. They even found a $50 refrigerator for me at a yard sale. Shirtless and sweaty, they pushed that thing up the street on a dolly. But even their love and friendship wasn't enough for me to feel like my life was moving in a positive direction. I was stressed out and going nowhere.

Becky knew just how down I was. Nothing seemed to bring me any joy. The only glimmer of happiness was when The Boys would tell me about the pyramid scheme they were involved in. There were secret parties where people would give envelopes of cash to the person at the top of their pyramid. The chart was shaped like a triangle with that one lucky person at the top. Each person at the bottom of the chart would discreetly hand $2,000 to the person who had made it all the way through the pyramid.

The Boys had made $48,000 and got a cash lockbox at the bank to keep their money in. Becky decided the only way to distract me through this difficult time with Cheating Charlie was to send me $2,000 to enter it myself. Somehow, she managed to send it. I never asked her where she got the money from. She just made me promise her that I'd go to the next pyramid scheme party with Paul and Eddie to try my luck. And so I did.

It was very exciting. And secretive. Not just anybody could go. You had to be invited by someone who was already involved. The Boys and I would dress up and go to big cocktail parties with our pyramid charts in hand. When someone tapped me on the shoulder, I stepped into the corner (of course, The Boys came with me) and I handed a stranger an envelope with two thousand cash in it. I had never had that much cash in my hand before. Could I have done something more responsible with that money? Of course! But I promised Becky!

The pyramid turned out to be a great distraction. The glamour. The cash. The covert operation. It was all intoxicating. This was going to be the easiest $16,000 I'd ever make!

Unfortunately, I was doomed from the start. I was supposed to bring in others to join the pyramid, but my friends didn't have that kind of cash. I was too soft-hearted to be a schemer. Someone asked me if they should get a loan from a family member so they could buy in.

"Oh my god, no." I'd say. "This isn't a sure thing. I'm pretty sure it's illegal. Don't get your loved ones involved!"

I worried about my recruits losing their money. I stopped telling potential "investors" about Paul and Eddie's windfall because I didn't want them to get roped in. Becky would call me all the time to hear updates. She was gleeful to hear about my little adventure.

The only friend I could find that could afford this risky venture was Brad, an old friend from my *Psycho* days who had joined the LA grind. I strutted into one of the parties with Brad and The Boys. I was on top of the world. We had the time of our lives—going to fancy parties, dancing, and dreaming about trips we might take with our upcoming winnings.

That was, until my pyramid stall. Even Paul and Eddie didn't want to join my pyramid. "No Cheryl. You're awful at this. You don't have enough hustle. There's no way we're going to give you $2,000," Paul said. "We worked too hard for our money."

Needless to say, I never reached the top. I never got to tap a stranger's shoulder to pull them aside and collect my cash. I had to tell Becky I'd lost her money. "Cher, I knew I'd never see that money again. It's a friggin' pyramid scheme," she said.

Somehow, the failure of my pyramid brought Becky and me hours and hours of entertainment.

I'd just like to take this opportunity to say, thank you, Brad. And I'm sorry.

Chapter 5

A call from the Groundlings with an invitation to perform in the Sunday company caused a seismic shift in my life. I was finally able to start writing sketches and performing in front of a live audience.

Casting directors and agents would flood the Sunday show to find up-and-coming talent. It was the perfect way for influential industry executives to see new talent. It put me on a path to finding an agent. Our director, Tony Sepulveda, and my castmates inspired me to new levels of creativity. I was working with top-tier comedians, performing with people like Will Forte, Maya Rudolph, Oscar Nuñez, and many, many others. Our number one goal was to make each other laugh at Wednesday night rehearsal. I soaked in everything I could from those brilliant performers as they all became close friends.

We created strong bonds that were true and authentic. We laid our souls bare as we wrote comedy sketches based on our painful relationships, embarrassing moments, and outrageous family members. I learned what made audiences laugh; they laughed because we were able to articulate life's absurdities. It was a masterclass in anthropology, psychology, comedy, and vulnerability.

As much as I resented Paul's peanut butter story, it sparked me to write one of my favorite sketches. My character was suing the cookie company where she worked because she had gotten salmonella. It was a trial scene, and I was on the stand. Kevin Ruf, a real lawyer, played the attorney. Ruf was one of the funniest cast members. He asked me if I had eaten any of the raw cookie dough while I was working.

"No," I said shyly but confidently as I leaned down to the microphone.

"Well, we actually have footage from our security camera that proves otherwise," he said.

With a click of a button, he showed a grainy video of me, half naked, covered in raw cookie dough. My boyfriend, played by the hilarious, overly serious Steve Pierce, wearing nothing but an apron, shoved raw cookie dough into his mouth and then kissed me wildly and sloppily until my mouth was full of cookie dough. The sketch was a crowd pleaser.

Every person on that stage was exceptional. In improv, you have to trust your scene partner. You're up there with no script, no props, and no idea what suggestion the audience is going to throw at you. The trick is to say *yes* to whatever information they give you *and* add on to it to create a scene. I was doing an improv with my friend Christine, and the director asked the audience what the scene was about. Someone yelled out "arsenic." The lights go down and then come up immediately to indicate the scene is starting.

"The house is on fire!" Christine yelled.

Well, I knew—and the audience knew—she thought the scene was about arson. I had to justify her idea that the house was on fire *and* convince her that she had just been poisoned.

"You're probably not going to have enough strength to drag yourself out in time because of that tea I just served you," I said as I looked at her intensely.

Eye contact is another key to improv. She could see that I was saying something important.

"I *am* starting to feel weak," she dropped to her knees and put her hands on her throat. "But that smell of gasoline is coming from your shoes. I soaked them while you were sleeping last night."

"You're trying to kill me!" I screamed.

"You're trying to kill *me*!" she screamed back.

Suddenly the scene was about two premeditated murders. The more she went on about fire, the more the audience howled. There's no such thing as mistakes in improv.

I especially loved writing with the brilliant Will Forte and Ken Polk. We wrote a farcical sketch about my boyfriend meeting my mother for the first time. (This was inspired by my real mom who horrified her children by "drip drying" in the nude after a shower. In her defense, it is really hot in Florida and there's no sense in putting on that final layer until you absolutely have to. But, maybe a bra and underwear wouldn't have killed her.)

Ken played my mother, who was wearing nothing but a silky robe and asked Will, my boyfriend, to rub some salve on her scar. With his back to the audience, Ken dropped his robe as Will, ointment in hand, stared blankly at her mother's naked body while I stood frozen with embarrassment.

"You can start here," Ken said as he pointed to his different body parts, "and work your way down past the left breast, loop around my bellybutton to my pelvic region—you can see the scar just grazes my bikini line, then it runs back up to my right nipple, circles around and down my right leg, to the back of my thigh, goes up right between my cheeks, comes back around, cuts into my nether region and ends on my hip," Ken explained in his best Southern drawl.

The time and care we took writing about that fictitious scar really had us going.

Amidst the laughter, Will said, "Can we just stop and hug each other for a second because it just doesn't get better than this."

That group hug in a sweaty West Hollywood apartment was the epitome of happiness. Maybe that memory is etched in my mind because it captured the spirit of who we were or maybe it's because Will had serendipitously created a perfect moment for us before Ken, suddenly and tragically, passed away a few months later.

I learned to really appreciate the little moments that brought me joy. I'd bank it in my "happiness silo" so I could access it later when I needed to remind myself that, just like grief and pain, happiness doesn't wait until you think you're ready to receive it. It comes in the shape of people, accomplishments, knowledge, and understanding, just waiting to be noticed.

***

The Groundlings could be a competitive place because there were always scouts for sketch shows in attendance. Everyone wanted to stand out. You have to trust that when you're up there performing, your scene partner is not going to sabotage you just to make themselves look good. That can happen, but for us it was a place where we would know that, if someone was coming to look at a certain person, even though you might feel envious, you're still excited for that person and you want them to stand out and be great. You want them to get that agent or that audition or that role, so there has to be mutual trust.

The people I was performing with were rock solid. They would always make me look good, and I believed they wanted the best for me. I felt the same about them. It was exciting because you would watch people being flown to New York to audition for SNL, see them get a great agent or book a job on a sitcom. Even when it didn't have to do with me, I'd think, "Oh, I'm in the mix for something and if I keep working hard, stay focused, and keep on this path, I know it's going to lead me somewhere good."

By then, I had found my way back to myself. I had a good sense of who I was and had the chance to build back my self-esteem. I was with people I trusted.

It was an exhilarating time. The show attracted all kinds of celebrities and influential people: Vince Vaughn, John Kennedy Jr., Christopher Guest. At the time, I was working for Rob Reiner, and he and his wife Michele would come to the shows, which I found incredibly supportive. I was witnessing other Groundlings like Will Ferrell, Cheri Oteri, Chris Kattan, and Chris Parnell skyrocket. Lisa Kudrow was on *Friends* and Mindy Sterling was in *Austin Powers*.

I felt that I was close to something, but not quite there. I kept getting called back for the sketch show, *Mad TV*, but they didn't offer me the part. Eventually, I had to quit working for the Reiners. It was too hard to keep taking time off for auditions and callbacks.

I started to book small roles on sitcoms. I even got a few lines on *Friends*! It was great, but I wasn't making enough to pay my rent. As the weeks went by, I started to become more and more desperate for a way to earn money to pay my bills. Becky was starting to worry about me. She knew I was running on fumes. She called.

"Hey, I sent you my ATM card so you can withdraw some cash. You've got to hang in there, Cher," she said reassuringly.

"What? Rebecca! You didn't have to do that," I told her.

"I know you're dying out there. Check your mail. It should be there," she said.

"Oh my god, thank you. I can't believe you did that."

And there it was. An envelope postmarked Orlando, Florida, with Becky's ATM card. I ran to the closest bank. I inserted the card, typed in the PIN, and requested $40. *Insufficient Funds.* Hmmm, I guess I was asking for too much. I requested $20. *Insufficient Funds.* I laughed so hard it annoyed the people waiting behind me. That's my sister! She'd give me the last dollar she had—if she had one. I just imagined her going through the trouble of going to the post office and mailing me that card. It didn't matter that she had no money in her account, the gesture alone made me feel so loved. I called her back.

"Hey, I tried your card, but I couldn't get any money out," I told her.

We laughed for a long time.

"Why would you send me a card if you didn't have any money in your account?"

"Well, it's always a crapshoot. Try it again next week on Friday. I might have some money by then," she said.

I sent the card back to her. I wasn't going to take her last dollar, but man, did I love her pluck.

I was barely scraping by and was looking for ways to stay inspired to keep me focused. I loved watching stand up, but I didn't have enough money to actually go to a club, so one Saturday night I called The Improv.

"Listen, I can't afford to pay the door charge, but I can scrape together enough for the two-drink minimum if you'll just let me in," I said.

The poor guy answering the phone said, "Who are you? What are you talking about?"

"My friends and I, we just can't . . . Well, I can't afford to buy tickets. But we are really good laughers. We're really loud. We'll be the best audience you've ever seen."

"Oh, God. Okay. Just come to the door and ask for Bill. I'll see what I can do," he said.

We went and laughed our asses off as promised. That's pretty much how I got by for the next few years.

My roommate Maria turned out to be a lifeline for me. She loaned me money for rent and a little extra to buy food when I couldn't afford it. To this day, we're as close as ever. We've traveled to Santorini and back and have been to every Hollywood party that would have us. I had found an angel in the City of Angels.

Maria's generosity was a temporary Band-Aid at the time but didn't stop the bleeding. My anxiety about money became more and more intense. I was performing in the Sunday company at the Groundlings, doing my best to write new sketches every week. I was sitting on the news that Larry asked me to play the role of his wife on a new show, but couldn't move forward until I had an official offer from HBO. My anxiety steadily amplified as the weeks turned into months.

***

In my final Sunday show, I did a sketch with Rachael Harris. I met Rachael at the theater, and we realized we were kindred spirits. She's one of the funniest, most talented actresses I know, and she's my true ride-or-die. Thinking about that sketch still makes me smile. We were in a college marching band: I played the tuba, she had the cymbals. As the band blared through a football game, we sat in the stands and tried to have a heartfelt conversation about how bittersweet it felt to be nearing the end of college.

We're baring our souls, mid-sentence, and the band bursts into the school fight song. I'd suddenly blast the tuba, Rachael would crash the cymbals, and we'd both yell, "Let's go Knights!" Then, just as abruptly, we'd drop back into our quiet existential dread about life after graduation. With each interruption, our frustration grew—until we were practically shouting over the music, trying to make sense of the future.

Was it the best sketch we ever did? Probably not. But it cracked us up. I remember that night especially because Martin Short was in the audience. After the show, we spent hours obsessing over whether he'd laughed. We never figured it out, but it was the beginning of a deep friendship that has weathered life's loud, unexpected disruptions.

It was a simpler time.

**

I shot the Larry David Special while I was still in the Sunday Company. When I showed up for the *Curb* shoot, I had no idea what to expect. There were no lines, no script, and no rehearsals. I just appeared on the set. Larry told me the special was about him trying to get back into stand-up. We started shooting and after his stand-up set, I said, "You know, that was pretty good. I just have a few notes."

He looked at me, annoyed, and laughed in irritated disbelief. "You're giving me notes?" he asked.

Jeff Garlin played Larry's manager, Jeff Green, perfectly. I immediately liked him from the moment we met. The special blurred the lines of reality as it followed Larry's journey with appearances by his real-life celebrity friends Richard Lewis, Jerry Seinfeld, Carol Leifer, and Jason Alexander.

After we shot the special, before it aired, I was still teaching and performing at the Groundlings. One of the Groundlings came up to me and said,

"Hey, I heard the Larry David special you did is going to become a TV show."

"Oh, I haven't heard that," I said.

"Yeah, I'm pretty sure it's happening," she said.

"Well, nobody's told me about it," I told her uncertainly, "but thanks for letting me know."

It didn't seem like a good sign for me. I tried not to think about it as I began auditioning for pilots—bigger projects that could make a difference in my life. There was a lot of pressure attached to those auditions. They often required me to perform in front of LA's top casting directors and then test in front of network executives. I would show up to a studio test and see two other actresses there for the same part. Even though we all desperately wanted the role, we'd find comfort in each other's presence and wish each other well. It was still nerve-racking.

I asked a casting director once if it was difficult casting TV pilots. She told me it could be really stressful. With films, studios usually offer the leads to established movie stars. But leading roles on a new show could completely change the life of an unknown actor.

***

One Sunday after our Groundlings performance, an excruciating pain in my back told me I needed medical care. I didn't have health insurance, so I called around to different emergency rooms shopping for a deal. Okay, $200. I didn't have it, but I'd deal with that later. I drove myself to a hospital in East LA. I had low expectations for the cheapest emergency room in LA, but the twelve hours before I got my first attention had me lowering the bar even further.

They made me put all of my belongings in a locker because they didn't want the responsibility for loss or theft. They took my purse and my clothes. Fortunately, I brought a paperback book with me because I suspected a long wait. At first, they insisted on taking the book and only succumbed to my pleas when I promised that I would be okay if someone took it.

I finally made it to a gurney, which they parked in the hospital hallway for another five hours. I finished the book and then just counted ceiling tiles until someone came and got me.

When I finally saw a doctor, he didn't want to give me anything for pain, in case my appendix burst, but he wasn't certain it was the problem. If that happened, I would be sent straight into surgery.

They finally put me in a ward with five other women. There were no curtains between us, just six hospital beds in a U shape. There was one payphone by the nurses station that required change to make a call.

No one knew I was there, not even my roommates. I hadn't wanted to burden them with worries about me in the emergency room. I asked one of the nurses if I could borrow a quarter so I could call Maria.

"What? Why didn't you tell me? I would've gone with you," she said. "What's happened?"

"No one seems to know exactly what the problem is, but it's nothing to worry about," I told her.

"I'm coming there right now."

"Maria, bring quarters. As many as you can find. I need your laundromat stash. Please," I begged.

The doctors were still scratching their heads and wanted to keep me overnight. Maria appeared with Paul and Eddie. When they walked in, Eddie was terrified. But Paul couldn't stop laughing. It seemed like I was in an asylum, and it felt that way. It was a teaching hospital, so every once in a while, ten or more people would come out of nowhere, surround my bed and ask me questions. *Are you in pain? Where does it hurt? How long has this been going on?* They would look at me and nod knowingly before disappearing. The interns' suggestions ranged from a kidney infection to appendicitis. They kept keeping me for "one more night."

There were no televisions, no reading lights, no nothing. Just an overhead light that the nurse would switch off at 10 p.m. I began questioning reality. I started to think that maybe I *had* had a psychotic break and had been committed to this asylum. I kept from despair by thinking about my life and remembering all of the good times. I kept telling myself that I would get out soon.

My Groundlings friend Steve rattled me with deep concern. He pulled up a chair about two inches away from my hospital bed and silently stared at me intently.

"I'm actually really tired. I think I'm gonna sleep for a while," I said. "Thanks so much for coming to see me."

"No problem," he said.

I closed my eyes for a few minutes, opened them and found Steve still staring at me.

"What are you doing?" I asked.

"I'm worried about you," he said.

"Well, you can't just sit here and watch me sleep for hours."

"Yes, I can," he said.

That really made me laugh.

"Steve, I'm going to be okay. You can't just sit here in this room full of women and watch me sleep."

"Well, let me just do it for a little while. I need to know that you're going to be okay."

"All right," I said, drifting off to sleep.

When I woke up, what seemed like hours later, Steve was still there, eyeballing me.

"Oh my God! Steve!" I said.

"Okay, I guess I'll go now," he said, getting up to leave.

I had a lot of time to spend with the other five women in my room. Mostly, we hashed out the medical problems that had landed us there. One of them asked me what I did for a living. I told her I was an actress. I explained that I had just been cast on an HBO show.

"As a matter of fact, I also have a small role on *Friends* that airs this Thursday." I said.

I could tell they didn't believe me.

"I'm just waiting for the official offer from HBO. I'm surprised it hasn't come in yet, but it should happen any minute." I reassured them.

"That sounds exciting," Patient #2 said skeptically.

Patient #4 was more direct. "So you want us to believe you're a television star?"

"Oh no, I'm not saying that, I'm just saying I'm going to be on a new show." I responded.

"But you're also on *Friends*?" Patient #5 asked.

"It's just a small part. An under five. Five lines or less. Although I did have to audition several times before I actually booked a part so, it's a pretty big deal for me." I said.

"I do like that show, *Friends*," Patient #6 chimed in.

"Uh-huh. That's a good show," said Patient #2.

After a while, the conversation just petered out. There were no starts and stops to our small talks because no one was ever getting up and leaving the room. The only real escape from the listless dialogue was pretending to fall asleep. Once in a blue moon, the welcomed arrival of a nurse would bring a merciful punctuation to the discussion.

When my friends would visit, I begged for quarters for the payphone. On Wednesday, I wheeled my IV down the hall with my ass flapping in the breeze of my hospital gown and called my agent to see if he had heard anything from HBO. "They finally just made the offer!" I was so happy not even the pain from my kidneys or my appendix or whatever it was, could prevent me from wheeling myself back into the asylum to inform the ladies.

"Well, it happened! The offer just came in from HBO!"

I might as well have said I was just named the queen of England.

"You already told us you were on a show," Patient #5 pointed out.

"We talked about this yesterday," said Patient #6.

"Right, but I said I was waiting for the *official* offer to come in. And it just did. I mean, it's really low. I won't go into it, but it's not a great offer. But I guess I'm not really doing it for the money, right? Although I do need to pay my bills. I'm still paying off my student loans. Anyway, I'm assuming there will be some sort of negotiation happening. And it's just really exciting to be on HBO," I said.

They just stared. I turned to the woman who had been given a tiny TV by a family member, "This is all true. You can watch *Friends* tomorrow night, and you'll see me."

She nodded her head yes. And that was that.

I was hoping I would be released from the hospital Thursday morning, but no such luck. Thursday night rolled around and I was still there. The woman with the tiny, portable TV was also still there.

"If you watch *Friends* tonight, you should see me. I'm at the end of the show. In the tag," I reminded her.

I watched the clock until 5:30 rolled around. I wheeled myself to the payphone and called Becky. I knew she had just watched the show in Orlando.

"Hey, what did you think?" I asked.

"Well, Reese Witherspoon is guest starring on next week's episode and they showed a clip of her instead of you. They cut the tag. Sorry, Cher," she said.

Oh boy. This was a new low. I rolled my IV back into the room. I didn't bother telling the ladies about my part being cut or about Reese Witherspoon starring on next week's episode. I just went back into my bed and lay there until I heard the woman next to me watching *Friends*. I listened to the whole episode, we all did, and just like Becky had said, they cut the tag at the end, and I was nowhere to be found in that episode. I didn't bother to explain. Nobody in the room asked me about it. It was just another night in the cozy hospital room for six.

I was finally released the next day. I went home with medication for a kidney infection. I wished the ladies well and retrieved my belongings from the locker. Maria took me back to our apartment. I couldn't have been happier.

Cheryl Hines

To this day, I've never seen the episode of *Friends* that I'm on, but I know it's out there in syndication. Every once in a while, I'll get a text from a friend saying, *Hey. I just saw your* Friends *episode!*

***

I had all my friends—Paul and Eddie, Maria and Mandy, and my friend Sarah packed into my tiny West Hollywood apartment to watch the *Curb Your Enthusiasm* premiere. It aired in the best time slot imaginable, right after *Sex and the City* and before *The Sopranos*.

That became our Sunday night ritual. Every week, my friends would come over, and we'd all watch the show together.

"Why are we in this shitty little apartment? You're on an HBO show—after *Sex and the City*, before *The Sopranos*. This is the best you can do?" Mandy asked.

We laughed about it. It *was* kind of crazy that I was still in my little place. But things were looking up. I was still in debt, but I bought a new, used car and finally paid off my student loans.

One of our favorite things to do back then was yard sales. Maria and I would set up beach chairs, sit in the sun, and chit chat with potential customers all day.

"How much for the wallet?" a girl asked.

We had gone to great lengths to price everything with stickers.

"Let's see, five dollars," I told her.

"That's kind of high," she haggled.

"Well, it's brand new."

"I don't know. Seems like it's too much," the guy with her said.

"I think we're gonna pass," as they walked off, he turned around and said, "by the way, we love you on *Curb*."

"Oh, thanks," I said and waved goodbye.

I couldn't wait to tell Larry the story. I thought he'd be amused that the guy watched *Curb*.

"Let me ask you something. How much did you make at that yard sale?" he asked.

"I don't know. Probably seventy-five dollars?"

"Next time you're thinking of having a yard sale, call me. I'll give you $75 to *not* have a yard sale. You can't be out there selling wallets on the side of the road," Larry said.

Chapter 6

I adored Larry from the moment I met him. I found him to be charming in a way I didn't know a person could be charming. He finds humor in how people navigate the unwritten rules and social conventions that govern everyday life. He scribbles comical incidents in a tiny leatherbound notebook that he always carries in his pocket. His ability to craft those anecdotes into complete plotlines that always merge into perfectly tied ribbons at the close of each episode is genius. Above all, he's authentic, intelligent, kind, very, very funny, and an immensely loyal friend.

The show was supposed to feel like the audience was a fly on the wall, watching Larry navigate through the ins and outs of his daily life as a successful TV show producer and writer, continually exasperated by the baffling norms of customs, manners, etiquette, and belief systems. It was, in essence, a mockumentary similar to the one-hour special. The show wasn't meant to look polished or highly produced. We didn't have a hair *and* a make-up team at that point. Larry had just one woman, Saundra, doing it all.

In Season 1, the most talented comedic actress on the planet, Julia Louis-Dreyfus, guest starred as herself. As an industry standard, she brought her own hair/make-up team and between takes, they would run onto the set and give Julia touch ups. To keep up appearances, Saundra would follow them out, to dust my face with a big, fluffy brush. "I'm just going to do this until they leave so you feel taken care of too," she whispered to me.

I loved Saundra. There was no better crew in the industry than the *Curb* crew. Saundra would try to sneak in a new hairstyle for me every so often. One time, she put tiny braids in my hair, but Larry wasn't having it. *Who does that?* Saundra did her best to convince Larry that French women do it every day, but Larry won that battle. No braids, no specific hairdo. Larry wanted everything to be as real as possible. He insisted on wearing his own clothes. I had to persuade him that I actually *did* need some sort of wardrobe for my character as Cheryl David. The costume designer showed him pajama options for me. One was a silky, slip-like nightgown.

"Nobody wears that to sleep in," he said.

"I do," I said.

"You wear that to sleep in?"

"Yeah. I don't have air conditioning so sometimes it gets hot," I told him.

"Well, it doesn't work for the show."

I ended up in a long-sleeve shirt and pajama pants. My mom would watch the show and say, "I wish you'd get a makeover. You look kind of frumpy."

The first day of shooting, I was in the dark about what we were doing. There was no telling what the episodes were about because there was no script. Larry had written a three- or four-page outline, but allowed only the producers and directors to see it. I found myself asking Larry questions in scenes as he would recount something offensive he had done earlier that day. As an improv teacher, I was always reminding my students of one of the golden rules of improv: don't ask questions, only add information. Oftentimes, though, it would be the first time I was hearing what Larry had done, and it usually didn't make sense to me. I would catch myself asking him, *Why in the world would you do that? Why would you trip Shaquille O'Neal during a Laker's game? Why are you asking me to bake brownies laced with Benadryl?*

In that first scene, it seemed like we just talked back-and-forth aimlessly all day. Then I went home. It felt so fun and easy, but I had little inkling of what the show was actually about. I knew Larry really made me laugh, but I wasn't sure if other people were gonna be as entertained as I was. In the middle of the scene, as he was talking, he picked up an apple and bit into it.

"This is kind of mealy," he said.

"Okay, well don't eat it." I said.

"Why do we have mealy apples?" he asked.

"How am I supposed to know if an apple is mealy or not?" I retorted.

"Are they all mealy?" he asked.

"Larry, I have no idea. Probably not. Just throw that one away and try another one," I suggested.

This exchange went on for a while. I wondered what lines Larry was going to leave in for the show and what lines he would edit out. Was the apple part of the story in the show? I wouldn't know until I watched it when it aired.

My friends made up a drinking game—everytime I said *Larry* on the show, they would take a drink. They threw back a lot of tequila in a thirty-minute window. And, no, the mealy apple didn't make it into "The Pants Tent" episode. It was probably better that I barely knew Larry. It gave me the advantage of genuine surprise when he revealed yet another of his idiosyncrasies. When he sat on the couch, he pointed to his crotch to show me how his pants bunched up making it look like he had an erection. Imagining what his wife would do, I poked it, "It's just material."

Another rule of improv is to assume a relationship, so that's what I did. I only learned later that Larry has issues about people touching him. I'd been told that he didn't want anyone touching him during the audition. But I didn't know that he doesn't even like shaking hands. He recoils from intrusions on his personal space. In one episode when he accidentally drinks out of Mary Steenburgen's mother's glass, Larry gags when he discovers his mistake.

On and off set, he would offer his elbow in lieu of a handshake. He had large ambitions of getting everyone to elbow touch as a standard greeting.

In the special, we were supposed to have kids. Larry mentioned that he couldn't attend an acquaintance's stepfather's wake because he had to go to his daughter's school for pizza night. But when we started the series, Larry decided it would be better if we didn't have kids in the show. We never spoke of kids again until Season 5, Episode 10, when Larry learns that he's adopted. He tells me he wants to have lots of kids because he wouldn't be passing on what he thought were his parents' genes.

Larry never showed the actors the episode outlines because he wanted the dialogue of *Curb* to be genuinely improvised. He said he would be distracted if he had lines to remember. He would be thinking about when to say his next line instead of being in the moment. He had a stripped-down approach to acting. He'd tell me that actors made the basic skill of acting sound hard and unnecessarily complex. He said, *"It's not that hard. If your stomach is supposed to be hurting, you just grab your stomach and say—Oh, my stomach hurts."*

Most of the time, the producers wouldn't even tell me the subject of the show. They'd just say, Larry's gonna come home and tell you what he did at the basketball game. We started shooting the scene and Larry mentioned that he had tripped Shaquille O'Neal during the Lakers game. Shaq had to be taken off the court by medics. I had a hard time not breaking. Many, many times I'd bite the inside of my cheek, Hightower style, to keep from ruining the take.

* * *

"What should your name be in this?" Larry asked me on that first day of shooting.

"I don't know." I said,

"Well, let's just call you Cheryl," he said.

"Okay," I replied.

"You know, I got sued by a guy named Costanza," he said.

"Oh, I didn't know that," I said.

"George Costanza was based on me," he insisted.

"Of course. That seems pretty obvious," I said.

"Okay, so you'll just be Cheryl David."

"Great, yeah, I'll just be Cheryl David."

When *Curb* came out, a lot of people thought I was married to Larry in real life. The casting director at one audition said, "Oh, you're also an actress."

"Also an actress?" I asked.

"I know you're doing the reality show with your husband, Larry," he said.

I explained that it wasn't a reality show and I wasn't actually married to Larry.

"Oh my god. How did I get that so wrong?" he asked.

He was far from the only person who thought this. The mom of one of my high school friends called my mother and said,

"Well, Cheryl got married!"

"Cheryl's not married," my mom replied.

"I thought she married Larry David. I was wondering why I wasn't invited to the wedding," she laughed.

"It seems like she would've told me something like that," my mom joked.

When I went out in public, people would call me Cheryl and start talking to me. I would think, *how do I know this person? They seem to know me.* It wouldn't be until they'd say, *where's Larry?* that I'd realize they knew me from *Curb*. When my nephew Griffin was little, we went out to dinner and people kept coming up to us.

"How do you know so many people in this restaurant? Did you use to work here or something?" he asked.

"It's because I'm on a TV show," I said.

"Really? Can I watch it?" he asked.

"No, I don't think so. It's not for four-year-olds," I said.

Curb Your Enthusiasm wasn't meant to appeal to everyone, and it didn't. My mom would often tell me in her sassiest Southern drawl, that she didn't see anything funny about the show.

"I don't get it."

"That's okay, Mom. A lot of people say that," I'd tell her.

My mom was nevertheless grateful to Larry for casting me on *Curb*, and she wanted to thank him in person. When she came out to visit, we took Larry out to lunch. I suspected that it might be a little awkward. I was pretty sure she wouldn't "get" Larry.

"What goes on in Shell Point, Rosemary?" Larry asked.

"Well, we just had a shrimp festival," my mother said, enthusiastically.

"What happens at a shrimp festival?" Larry asked.

"Oh, it's a sort of shrimp celebration. There's all kinds of shrimp related things," she said again with that slow Southern drawl.

"Oh yeah? Like, what?" he asked.

"Well, there are arts and crafts with shrimp on it. Like potholders and dish towels with shrimp."

"What else?" he said.

"Well, they have shrimp eating contests," she went on.

"Is that so, Rosemary? What other kind of shrimp stuff happens at a shrimp festival?" he encouraged her.

"Let's see. Of course, there's lots of shrimp to eat. They have boiled shrimp, fried shrimp, cajun shrimp," she continued.

"Uh huh, what else?" He baited her as I kicked him under the table.

"Shrimp flavored ice cream, if you can believe that," she told him.

"I can't believe that, Rosemary, you're kidding?" he asked with feigned astonishment.

Larry asked one shrimp question after another until my mother was exhausted. As my mom and I walked to the car, I asked, "Well, what did you think of Larry?"

"He was nice, but he doesn't know a thing about shrimp!"

***

I had no idea religion would be part of the storylines on *Curb*. How could I have known? I didn't even know what I was auditioning for! On one of my first days on set, Larry or Richard said something in Yiddish.

"What does that mean?" I asked.

"Who's gonna believe you're Jewish?" Larry asked.

"Am I supposed to be Jewish?" I asked. I genuinely didn't know.

"Maybe you don't have to be," he said.

"Okay," I said,

"What are you?"

"I was raised Catholic," I told him.

"Well, maybe we'll just go with that."

"Sure," I shrugged.

When I went home to Florida for Christmas one year, my sister-in-law made a nativity scene out of cookies. There were sugar cookie versions of Jesus, Mary, and Joseph. The hay was toasted coconut. It was adorable.

The kids kept running in for snacks, and the adults sat talking around the kitchen table. Every few minutes you'd hear someone yell to the kids, "Nobody eat baby Jesus!"

I called Larry and said, "If you were here, you would eat baby Jesus, and my family would lose their minds."

"What else is going on down there?" He asked.

"Well, there are live nativity scenes," I said.

"What are you talking about?" he asked.

"It's Florida. People stand outside on their lawns—or on church lawns—dressed up as the nativity scene and do a sort of performance art for people passing by," I explained.

This sparked the "Mary, Joseph and Larry" episode in Season 3, Episode 9. My family comes to visit, and they've baked a nativity cookie scene. At one point, my sister, played perfectly by Kaitlin Olson (of course named Becky, on *Curb*) storms in and asks,

"Who ate baby Jesus?"

Larry had eaten baby Jesus *and* Mary. My fictitious family was furious. In an attempt to appease them, Larry enlists actors from a nearby church to perform a live nativity scene on our front lawn.

Pleased with his scene, Larry pulls Joseph (played hilariously by David Koechner) aside for a tete-a-tete.

"Joseph, let me ask you a question . . ." he starts.

Larry starts choking and coughing.

"You okay?" Joseph asks.

"I've got a pubic hair stuck in my throat," Larry matter-of-factly complains.

"Oh, that's unfortunate," Joseph says.

"I can't get rid of this thing. It's driving me nuts, Joseph. Driving me nuts," he says.

Larry looks over at a very attractive Mary.

"Oh boy, that Mary. By the way, has quite the bod," Larry continues.

"What?" Joseph asks.

"Come on, Joey, between you and me—you and Mary, huh? You don't feel like it every now and then? What do you do?" Larry asks.

"No. You know what? We're leaving. That's it. Let's pack it up," Joseph shouts out to the manger scene actors.

"What? Come on, Joe," Larry pleads.

"I'm not going to stand for this. Don't *Joe* me. We're leaving. You *will* take it back! We're leaving," Joseph starts to wrestle Larry to the ground.

"Get your hands off of me," Larry retaliates.

"You'll stand right here and take it back," Joseph says.

The wrestling continues and then Larry stops everything. "Wait a second," Larry yells as Joseph, Mary, and the shepherds look on, concerned. "The pubic hair. It's out!" Larry says, quite relieved.

Larry then looks up to see me, my mother, father, and sister looking down on him angrily. As usual, his best intentions have earned him the disgust of a hostile world.

***

People often ask me if Larry David is anything like his character on the show. His brilliance is his genius for tapping his neuroses as a rich wellspring of comedy. Then there are the times when he's just being himself, in real life, without an ounce of self-awareness. I went to lunch with him one day. A nice guy stopped for a moment at our table.

"Larry, we went to college together!"

"Oh, okay, yeah, good to see you," Larry says.

We sit down, and Larry says, "I really have to use the bathroom."

"Well, go to the bathroom, Larry," I said.

"Is that guy still sitting there?" he asked.

"Yes."

"I'll wait," he said.

"Why would you wait?" I asked.

"I don't want to go through it all again. I'd have to walk by his table. He's gonna stop me and want to talk," Larry complained.

"So? Just nod and walk by quickly," I advised.

"I'm not doing that. I'll just wait until he leaves," he said.

We started talking and eating. . . .

"Is he still there?" Larry asked again.

"Oh my God, Larry, just go to the bathroom!"

"No, I won't! Just tell me when he leaves."

That was the whole lunch. All we talked about was the guy, when he might leave, and if Larry should go out the backdoor and use the bathroom in the coffee shop next door. Ultimately, Larry opted for the coffee shop.

***

Also endearingly neurotic, was Richard Lewis. In my twenties, from afar, I had the biggest crush on Richard. I was enamored with his sense of humor and loved watching him perform on stage, running his hands through his hair as he paced around, mining laughs from his bottomless angst. I was beside myself when I got to work with him. The actors on *Curb* were such characters themselves. The moments when the cameras weren't rolling were often the funniest.

Larry didn't want any of the actors to think about what they were going to say in a scene beforehand. He wanted spontaneity. We never rehearsed anything or even discussed the scene until we were rolling. That drove Richard crazy. One time, Larry and I were making small talk, dawdling on set as the cameras got ready to shoot a scene. Richard, positioned across the room from Larry and me, yells at us loudly.

"What are you two talking about? Are you planning out what you're gonna say?"

"What? No. We're talking about lunch," Larry yelled back.

"No you're not. I know what you're up to!" Richard yelled.

Larry told me that's why he doesn't let anyone see the outline. He didn't want anyone trying to come up with funny lines before we started shooting. Larry would always call people out on it if he thought somebody was trying to go for a premeditated laugh. He'd say—in the middle of a scene—*"What? Why are you saying that? Did you think that up last night and you wanted to get it in?"*

Once, I invited the cast to a poker tournament at my house. Richard had never played Texas Hold'em and struggled with the idea of placing a blind bet before the cards were even dealt. The "blinds" rotate around the table, so everyone had to place blind bets when it was their turn. The routine triggered his paranoia. Every time Richard was the small blind or big blind, he'd go into a conspiratorial rant.

"What is this? How come I'm the only one putting money in? This is insane. I'd like to see my cards before I put my money in," he said as he ran his hands through his long, dark hair.

"Richard, everyone has been doing it. It goes around the table," I explained.

"What? I haven't seen anyone else doing this. You guys are taking advantage of me because I don't know how to play this game."

The other players badgered him to quit holding up the game and put his money in.

"I see what's happening. Let's get Lewis over here and take his money. I'm not doing it until I see my cards. I'm not a schmuck!"

He finally threw his money in, lost the hand, and began another rant about how we all had been plotting the whole night, trying to con $500 out of him. The cameras should've been rolling. It was, by far, the most entertaining game of poker I've ever played.

Besides being one of the most gifted comedians, Richard was also one of the sweetest souls I've met. Through the years, he'd randomly send me notes telling me how talented I was, how he valued my friendship, and how much he loved me. He turned out to be the person I had always imagined and so much more. I'm forever grateful I had the privilege of circling in his orbit.

***

When the show premiered, I asked Larry why he didn't talk about *Curb* being improvised in the press. I always thought it was interesting that we, uniquely, didn't have a script. Larry explained that he didn't want people watching the show because it's improvised, he wanted them to watch because it's a good show.

Ours was not a fancy production. Most shows have trailers or dressing rooms for each of the actors, but on *Curb*, Jeff, Larry, Susie, the director, the producers, and I all shared that one trailer. We shot on location, so we never had a soundstage or a permanent home base. We would just take our one trailer everywhere. It was perfect for us. All of those intimate conversations in our community trailer with some of the world's most gifted, fascinating people only made the experience more perfect.

We didn't have a lot of downtime because there were always at least two cameras rolling at the same time. Since the dialogue was improvised, there needed to be a camera on Larry and one on the person to whom he was speaking. No two takes were ever the same, so the camera and sound had to capture every change in all the action. A lot of time is spent now on typical TV or film sets lighting one side of a room, shooting the coverage from that side of the room and then taking a long break to flip the lighting and the cameras to capture the scene from the other side of the room. The most time we spent in the trailer was during lunch. It was because of our singular trailer set up that I had one of the most extraordinary lunches of all time.

We were filming, "Opening Night," Season 4, Episode 10, in New York, in which Larry stars in the Broadway production of *The Producers*. As usual, we gathered for lunch in our trailer. In that small space were Larry, Jeff, Jerry, David Schwimmer, Mel Brooks, and me, eating lunch off of paper plates between laughs. The only interruption was when Ann Bancroft breezed in to change in the small bedroom in the rear of the trailer. It seems like a dream now.

Larry and I wanted to see a play while we were in New York. We were trying to pick out a show when Jeff Garlin joined us. "You guys have to see *Mame*," Jeff said. (It wasn't actually Mame, but for the sake of the story, let's say it was.)

Neither Larry nor I were crazy about musicals. People breaking into song every other sentence made us both uncomfortable.

"We'd rather see a play," I told Jeff.

"No, you've got to see *Mame*. I just saw it. It's so good," he insisted.

I love Jeff. When he's excited about something, he wants to share it with you. As we continued our debate over which play to see, Jeff circled back around.

"Great news. I just got you guys tickets to *Mame* tonight. One of my friends is in it, so I made a call. It's all set. You're going to love it. I promise," Jeff said.

As Larry and I watched the first half, he was continuously shifting uncomfortably in his seat. He sighed and made little noises to make it clear he wasn't enjoying the show. At intermission, the lights came up, and he turned to me.

"I wish I could leave."

"I wish you would," I told him. "You should leave."

"Well, what if someone notices I left? I don't want them to think that I walked out of the show," he said. "It has nothing to do with the actors, they're great, it's just—all the singing and dancing. I can't take it."

"Please go. If anyone says anything, I'll tell them you weren't feeling well and had to leave."

So Larry slipped out while the lights were still up. I watched the rest of the show in peace. When the curtain dropped, the audience was on their feet, clapping wildly, in a standing ovation. And then, out of nowhere, Larry comes striding down the aisle and stands right next to me, clapping along with everyone else.

"Don't look at me. Just keep clapping," he whispered.

"Why are you here?" I whispered back.

"I went back to the hotel and Jeff saw me in the lobby and said, '*What are you doing? You're supposed to go backstage after the show. You've got to meet the cast,*'" Larry said.

"What?" I asked.

"Yeah, one of the producers is coming to get us right now. I had to take a cab back here." On cue, a man approached us.

"Can I take you backstage?"

"That would be great," I replied.

"How did you like it?" he asked.

"We loved it," I said.

"Yeah, yeah. Loved it," Larry affirmed.

***

In 2002, I guest starred on an episode of *Everybody Loves Raymond*. I got to work with Ray Romano, Brad Garrett, and Patricia Heaton. It was a completely different routine. I had some experience on multi-camera sitcoms as an "under five" on shows like *Friends*, *Suddenly Susan*, and *The Wayans Bros.*, all shot before live audiences. It had been a while, though, since I had acted in a big network production.

Everybody Loves Raymond was shot on a soundstage, and I marveled at how all the actors had their own dressing rooms. Patty Heaton was so kind to me. She invited me into her room for a minute to say hello. I couldn't believe how nice it was.

Unscripted

There was a lot of excitement on the *Raymond* soundstage. The actors would huddle together and do a speed run of their lines just before the show started taping. It was fun but a little stressful. There were so many people around while we were shooting, in contrast to our small, casual, *Curb* set. Writers sat off to the side with the show runner, Phil Rosenthal, surrounded by all the cameras and the cam operators; the lighting crew, and the audience. After every scene, the writers would huddle around to change a line or two or punch up a joke. Then the actors would perform the scene again to gauge the audience reaction.

On our *Curb* set, I was used to standing in the kitchen with Larry having intimate conversations. The director and producers watched the scenes on monitors from "Video Village," a production area in a different room in the house. Most of the time, it just felt like Larry and I were standing around talking and there happened to be a TV crew capturing our conversation.

For many years, *Curb* would be nominated for Emmys and Golden Globes along with big studio shows like *Everybody Loves Raymond, Frasier, Sex and the City, Arrested Development, Will & Grace,* and *Desperate Housewives*. I couldn't believe the contrast between our low budget operation and the grand industrial enterprise that goes into creating most other sitcoms.

***

The *Curb* set was nearly always light and fun. I adored working with Susie and Jeff. I can't remember having a bad day working on the show. There was a lot of love and lots of laughs. There was only one time I remember real tension on the set.

Ben Stiller was guest-starring, and we were filming in a theater downtown. There was a lot going on that day, including an array of extras, which was unusual for us. We'd already shot a scene where Larry and I ran into Ben and his wife, Christine. Larry had a bandage on his head that was part of the story. The next day we finished shooting the theater scene with Ben and Christine. I was on the 101 freeway, headed home, when I got a call: "You have to come back."

"What's going on?"

They told me Larry didn't have the bandage on his head in any of the shots. "Oh, no," I said. "That's not good."

Everyone was trying to figure out how we missed it.

When I got back to the theater, the entire crew was wearing Band-Aids on their foreheads in solidarity. As if to say, "Yep, we all messed up." It was really sweet. A little chaotic, but sweet.

Larry is often angry on *Curb*, but in real life I've rarely seen him mad. Yes, he has an irritable disposition—annoyed by people and even more impatient with social norms—but his dominant character trait is his deeply caring nature. He took me aside after I returned home from visiting my nephew Michael in Florida. It was a particularly frightening time because Michael had been hospitalized, which was a relatively common occurrence because of his intensive health needs, but this time he was fighting for his life. I was there with my family as we rallied around him during his recovery.

Larry asked me how I was doing, and I told him I was fine. He asked how Michael was doing, and I told him he was doing much better and had returned home from the hospital. We talked for a few minutes about it and then he asked me how my family was holding up. I assured him everyone was doing okay.

"Okay, are we done? I can keep asking you questions, but it sounds like the family's okay, Michael's okay, you're okay. We can go on if you want, but are you good?"

"Yeah, I'm good."

Chapter 7

Three years after I started *Curb*, I met Paul Young, an entertainment manager and producer, through the Groundlings board of directors. I was on the board as a Groundlings member; Paul had a seat representing the business community. I was immediately taken with him. He was calm, smart, funny, driven, and handsome. Like me, he had come from humble beginnings. Through hard work, determination, good instincts, and a brilliant mind, he had built a successful Hollywood management company.

My family knew right away there was something different about Paul. They could see that our relationship was nothing like others I'd had in the past. When I went home for Christmas, my siblings and in-laws had wrapped predictions about our future and placed them under the tree. They had all placed bets on when I would marry Paul. We got married the following December. I think my sister-in-law, April, won the bet.

While Paul and I were dating, we took a trip to Moscow for the wedding of one of his friends. One of the wedding activities was a spirited paintball game. I'd been warned that a shot could leave welts on your skin. I had a few things going against me: I'd never played paintball before, I didn't speak a word of Russian, and I hated the thought of getting shot.

My strategy was to hide until it was over. We were in the middle of shooting *Curb*, so I didn't want to show up on set covered in red welts. Paul also was exercising caution, particularly after we learned that our opposing team included an ex-KGB agent. We crouched behind a big log for a long time as we listened to the guys shouting. We had a hard time knowing when the game was over because Paul also didn't speak a word of Russian. There were no signals, no announcements.

Finally, it was quiet, so Paul decided to raise his head just enough to see what was going on. Apparently, that ex-KGB member had him in his crosshairs. He was immediately shot between the eyes. The paint splattered across his goggles, and he left the field. I didn't move for another hour. There was no way out. *Do I pop up and just take the hit, or stay crouched here sweating my ass off in my utility jumpsuit?* Finally, I heard a lot of yelling. I could barely make out Paul's voice in the mix.

"Cheryl. You've got to come out. It's over! Everybody is waiting for you. Nobody's going to shoot you," he shouted.

I walked out slowly, with my hands up.

***

Early in my relationship with Paul, I got a call from my agent Bruce that *Curb* had been nominated for an Emmy. I knew it was huge, but I remember asking, "What does this mean? Am I going to walk the red carpet?"

"Yeah, of course—you're going to walk the red carpet. Your show's been nominated," Bruce said. I thought, *Wow. Okay. This is crazy.*

On the big night, Paul and I were so excited. It was our first time to the Emmy's for both of us, and everything I had dreamed of as a little girl. The hair stylist. The make-up. The designer gown. (Somehow the combo earned me spots on both the best dressed and worst dressed of the evening—but that's beside the point.) Paul, Eddie, and Sarah were so excited that they drove my Toyota Tercel as close as they could to the venue and climbed up a tree so they could watch me walk the red carpet.

That same year, we were nominated for a Golden Globe in comedy, and we won. I went up on stage with Larry and Jeff. It was surreal. Afterward, I was walking through the hallway and ran into Jeff Goldblum and Harrison Ford. They stopped to say, "Congratulations."

"Thank you," I said, holding out my hand. "Hi, I'm Cheryl Hines."

Harrison Ford said, "I know who you are."

Jeff said, "Yeah, we know who you are."

I thought, *What is happening in my life right now?*

***

When we started dating, Paul and I attended a very elegant New Year's Eve party, replete with endless bottles of expensive champagne. At some point, I couldn't drink any more champagne, so I discreetly walked outside, poured out my Dom Perignon and filled my champagne flute with Budweiser. When I returned to the party, Paul leaned over to me. "I saw what you did. I know what's in your glass," he laughed.

He told that story at our wedding, one year after that first New Year's Eve together. He had arranged a toast, complete with Budweiser for our champagne glasses. My mom also gave a toast, saluting my thirty-seven years of living single. "Well, I didn't think Cheryl would *ever* get married," she said in her exaggerated drawl. "I mean, she took a long, long, long time. I just can't believe she actually did it. Cheers y'all!"

We spent our honeymoon in Maui, and many hours in the hotel lounge. There was a Yahtzee game at the table, so, of course, we decided to play.

Beau Bridges, who neither of us knew but admired as an actor, was sitting a few tables behind us. We made up a rule that if you got Yahtzee, you had to turn around, look Beau Bridges in the eyes with intensity, and say, "Yahtzee." I'm sorry, Beau Bridges.

***

Becky was six months pregnant with twins at our wedding, and made a beautiful maid of honor, despite her cankles. Her legs were so swollen, we couldn't tell where her foot ended and her calves began. It wasn't her best look, but we could see the cankle humor.

I flew home to Florida not long after to be with her for the birth of the twins. I was with her in the operating room during her C-section. Neither of us was sure what to expect. As we're chatting and the doctors are making their first cuts, we look over only to see our brothers and their families, including the kids, peeking through the blinds of the viewing window. Somehow, they snuck into a closed observation room, and we had our very own viewing gallery. Becky and I burst out laughing.

"Don't let them see anything weird," she told me.

"Becky, they're seeing everything. A doctor is holding your intestines." I tried to make sure no private areas were showing. Frankly, the blood was covering most everything anyway.

We were laughing so hard, tears were streaming down our faces. "I've never had to say this during a C section before," the doctor said, "but Becky, you've got to stop laughing. It's not good for the babies."

Becky made it through the rest of the surgery without making a peep and our family welcomed Zoe and Jackson into the world.

My brother Chris and his wife, April, were also expecting a new Hines baby. Just six weeks after Becky's twins were born, Little Michael, named after our brother Mike, was born. Three months premature, he barely weighed two pounds, and Chris and April had a far different delivery experience. . . .

We all rushed to the hospital and sat, stunned into near silence, as we waited for Chris to come out and tell us what was happening. The news was stark. It was uncertain if Michael's lungs were going to develop fully enough for his survival. He spent his first three months in the neonatal intensive care unit. It was an unimaginably hard time for Chris and April, taking shifts at the Ronald McDonald house by the hospital to be with Michael while their other son, Griffin, stayed with Mike and my sister-in-law, Mary. Becky was managing her newborn twins, passing them off to Mike and Mary for a few hours when she could, so she could go see Michael. Chris, Becky, and Mike all lived on the same street at the time, and it was months, which became years, of sharing in the caretaking of kids.

Eventually, Michael was released from the hospital, and Chris and April were able to bring him home. By this time, it was clear that he would have many health struggles ahead. It was a challenging time for the family.

***

Eight months later, I also had a baby, my daughter, Cat. It was the greatest day of my life. I couldn't wait to see her little face.

My pregnancy wasn't like some of my friends', not exactly rainbows and butterflies. I found myself depressed and overwhelmed, which was a real change for me. I could stare at a wall and cry for eight hours straight.

Paul had a hard time navigating those emotional days. One time during my pregnancy, I came home from shopping, and I was in full, heaving tears.

"Oh my God. What happened?" Paul asked.

"The soldier goes off to war," I sobbed. "His boots are muddy, and he's waiting for a letter from home. Everyone's getting one, and he's not getting one."

"What?"

"There ain't nothing funny when a soldier cries, Paul."

"Is that a country song?" he asked.

"Yes, Paul, but it happens! It happens!"

"OK," he said. "I don't think you should listen to any more country music until after we have the baby."

In my hormonal despair, the only thing that kept me going was online poker. My friend, Sarah, taught me how to play Texas Hold'em, and I played nonstop. Behind a computer screen no one could see me cry as I raised and bluffed my way to win tournament after tournament. I had nine long months to hone my skills. It was the perfect pastime for me.

The moment Cat was born, I looked at her and all of my sadness and anxiety evaporated. No one was more relieved than Paul.

When I saw Cat's face for the first time, I was completely in love with her. I would hold her for hours, reading her stories and singing her country songs until she drifted off to sleep. Those quiet nights felt perfect, like the whole world had shrunk to just the two of us. Oh yeah, and Paul.

In those early years, I couldn't even imagine having another baby. The thought terrified me. I felt so certain that I could never love another child as much as I loved Cat. I remember thinking, *What would happen then? If I have another one, I'll always be stuck with the baby, and Paul will get to hold Cat.* It sounds harsh, but those were the kinds of thoughts I wrestled with in the middle of the night when the house was quiet and my mind wouldn't stop spinning.

Of course, I knew other people have more than one child. People do it every day. But I always thought, secretly, that parents probably liked one of them more than the others, and I knew—at least I thought I knew—that I would always like Cat more. It wasn't until years later, when I became a stepmom, did I understand that parents are able to love more than one child. You don't compare them, as I naively thought. Every child is different, so you have a unique love for each of them that's profound and life changing.

After seven years of marriage, it was clear that Paul and I made better friends than spouses. When we got divorced, we did it in the most considerate, loving way possible. We even took our rings off at the same time. If there's such a thing as a "nice" divorce, that was it. Paul and I have considered each other family and have remained very close as we both raised Cat together. Our relationship remained so close that my current husband, Bobby, became fast friends with Paul. Before he was remarried in 2022, Paul accompanied us on most of our vacations, skiing with us in the winters and summering with us at Cape Cod. We got divorced but we kept our family together. Cat and I have always been close in a way that's hard to describe. She can tell me everything. We've built that trust over years of late-night talks, car rides, and little moments that only the two of us share.

***

I was in LA when Michael was formally diagnosed with cerebral palsy, so I did the only thing I could think to do: I opened the yellow pages (I guess we still used them in 2005?)—and found United Cerebral Palsy in LA. I cold-called them and said, "Hi, I'm Cheryl Hines. My nephew was just diagnosed with cerebral palsy, and I don't know anything about it."

"Why don't you come in and meet with me? I can probably answer a lot of your questions," the friendly voice on the phone said.

I met with Ron Cohen, the CEO of UCP Los Angeles. He was so kind. I sat across from his desk, and he gently pushed a box of tissues toward me. I thought, *Why would I need tissues?* But then he explained: cerebral palsy usually occurs when there's a lack of oxygen during childbirth. It severs certain connections in the brain, so even if the brain tells the body to move, the message doesn't get through. It's not progressive, it doesn't get worse, but it also doesn't get better. He explained that it would be hard to know how much this would impact Michael, that the severity differs. I just sat there, stunned. I did need the tissues.

I called Chris and flew to Orlando. Ron connected me with Dr. Ilene Wilkins at UCP of Central Florida, and Chris and I took Michael to find out more information. During our visit we saw kids in wheelchairs, others using walkers, some nonverbal, some "typical"—playing, laughing, and just being kids. Michael, in his little wheelchair, and in spite of his other significant needs, had found his perfect preschool.

***

While I was navigating the early years of motherhood, it felt like a parallel universe. By now I had my real life where I was married and had a daughter, and then I had my TV life where I was married to Larry. Changes were happening with *Curb*, and there was a shift on the show when Larry and I got divorced. Once again, our break-up scene was inspired by real life.

I was talking to my friend Geraldine, and she told me about a comical experience she just had. She was on a plane, and the pilot came on the intercom with an announcement.

"We're having issues with the landing gear. We're not sure if the wheels are going to come down when we land, so we're going to circle for a while and dump fuel. We're expecting a rough landing," he warned.

Naturally, people started calling their loved ones. Many passengers were crying as they said their goodbyes. Geraldine called her husband to tell him about the situation and tell him she loved him.

"Can I call you back? I've been waiting all day for this technician, and he just got here," he said as he rushed her off the phone.

"No, I'm telling you, something's wrong with the plane," she said.

"Let me call you right back. This guy just got here," he said, distractedly.

I told Larry that story and the next thing I know, we're doing a version of it on *Curb*. In the episode, I'm on a plane, and I call

Larry to tell him we might be going down. He's with the TiVo guy, trying to save shows.

"I love you," I told him.

"Wait, what shows are we trying to save? *Barefoot Contessa*? Is that your show?" he asks.

I'm trying to say goodbye, and he's trying to prioritize Ina Garten.

Meanwhile, there's a guy sitting next to me on the plane, and during some turbulence, we touch hands and there was a strange, intimate moment between us.

When I get back, I tell Larry, "It's over. I can't stay with you anymore. I always tell people there's another side of Larry that you don't see, but really, there's not."

And that was the beginning of the end of our marriage. I remember thinking, *Oh, I just wrote myself out of* Curb Your Enthusiasm.

***

The good thing about my TV divorce was that it gave me time to focus on motherhood. Now, I can't say I was the perfect Los Angeles mom.

It took me a while to fit in with the other moms at Cat's school. I was supposed to make a dish reflecting our heritage for International Lunch Day. I made a delicious crockpot full of Irish stew. When I arrived at the school to drop it off, one of the moms said, "Great. We don't have any representation from Ireland, you can set up between Italy and Switzerland."

"Oh, I thought I was just dropping it off," I said.

"No, you'll need to serve it too," she said as she handed me a tiny flag of Ireland to put in front of my crockpot.

The other countries had three or four moms working on their giant, ornate displays of spaghetti and chocolate towers. I had to represent the entire country of Ireland by myself? I glanced over and saw the USA table. It was stacked high with cheeseburgers and french fries. USA? I didn't know that was an option! The school bell rang, and the kids ran out onto the lawn to see what fantastic treats we were serving. Cat ran up to my table.

"Hi mom! What *is* this?" she asked.

As I ladled out a few Dixie cups of brown goodness, I said to her and her friends, "This is Irish stew. My mom used to make it for me when I was little."

"Gross," one of her friends replied. "Whoa, look at Italy!"

Two seconds later, I watched my Italian neighbor pile meatballs and cannoli onto their plates. The kids were so happy. I had no takers in Ireland. Well, that's not entirely true, one of the PE coaches was drawn to my crockpot and absolutely loved my stew. He probably had twenty-five tiny cups worth.

I got my revenge on Career Day, though. Now I knew how this game was played. I set up my Actor's Booth with loads of popcorn and spent the day giving face paint tips as I'd draw whiskers and superhero masks onto the kids' faces. My line was the longest. I almost felt sorry for the banker next me with her business cards and pens but, sometimes you have to learn the hard way.

Sleepovers proved to be a little tricky too. The girls came over with their overnight bags, excited for the night and then one by one, they called their parents to come pick them up because "they had a stomachache." Maria came over to keep me company as we coordinated the handovers with parents. There was one tough girl that looked like she was actually going to make it through the night. Around midnight, she sleepily walked into the kitchen to see if anyone was still awake.

"Hi Kimberly. Are you okay?" I asked.

"Yeah, but I can't sleep," she said.

"Oh, are you afraid to fall asleep because you're scared someone will draw a moustache on you with a sharpie?" Maria asked.

She burst into tears.

"What? Is that what happens? Can you call my dad?"

Chapter 8

My online poker paid off. When I was able to sneak away from the house, I started playing poker in person. I met Suzanne Todd, a powerhouse producer with a perceptive sense of humor and a gift for bringing people together, at a party. Suzanne is a successful movie producer whose credits include *Austin Powers* and *Alice in Wonderland*. We quickly became friends and have navigated kids, careers, and marriages together through the years.

Shortly after meeting her, Suzanne invited me to her girls' poker game. I use the term "girls" loosely. We were middle-aged ladies. They were all witty and clever with a wide range of life experiences and accomplishments. They were also all very good players.

I had to up my game and get used to playing with real people. It threw me off when I would bluff and a few of the women would take it personally, like it was a betrayal of friendship. *How could you just look me in the eye and lie?*

Around this same time, Ray Romano invited me into his all-guys poker night. This group was mainly well-known comedians.

Big games were pure entertainment. In the women's game, we talked about friends, spouses, and children. In the guys' group, there was a lot of talk about football, cholesterol levels, and punchlines.

I started getting invited to play on *Celebrity Poker Showdown*, which was a very popular TV show. I had learned a lot from playing with my gifted friends, and I ended up head-to-head with basketball legend, Dennis Rodman. It was close, but I took him down. It was quite a show. I had a great time with Dennis, then I went on to the final tournament and ended up head-to-head with the late, great Alex Trebek. Somehow, I won it all. I was grateful to be able to donate my winnings to UCP.

My newfound poker prowess helped get me cast in an improvised comedic film called *The Grand*, which followed a big poker tournament in Las Vegas. The uber talented Zak Penn directed an amazing cast: Woody Harrelson, David Cross, Richard Kind, Chris Parnell, Jason Alexander, Ray Romano, and even Werner Herzog, the German documentary filmmaker. It was a crazy fun shoot. Cat, at the age of three, even made an appearance in the film during a hotel check-in scene.

My character was loosely based on the iconic poker player Annie Duke. She was always surrounded by guys and managed to hold her own. In the script, it was predetermined which ten players would make it to the final table, but once we got to the final table, Zak wanted us to really play to see who would get knocked out and who would win.

We each started with different chip stacks, so some players had an advantage. I had a medium stack. The actors who made it to the final table decided to throw in $100 as a side bet to make it interesting, so we were playing for $900 in real life, while our characters were playing for $10 million. Our pot was only $900 because Dennis Farina, who I adored, didn't want in on the bet.

He had 9:00 dinner reservations and was planning on busting out early. And he did.

It came down to heads up with me and Woody Harrelson. He's a great poker player and dominated the game with a nuanced comedic skill. I started gaining momentum, though, and could feel my luck changing. I wondered if it would make more sense in the film for Woody to win. During a break, I asked Zak if Woody should win. Zak told me to just keep playing my best. "Whoever wins, wins, and that will determine how the film ends."

We were heads up and I started to feel Woody getting aggressive, as players do when they're trying to take it down. He was raising, bluffing, trying to get me to fold, but I kept calling. I was pretty sure Woody didn't have good cards and was trying to bully me out. I got lucky and ended up winning. Like an obsessed poker player, I still couldn't stop wondering about Woody's cards.

After we wrapped, I asked Zak if I could watch the footage from those last few hands. It turned out, he *did* have good cards. He should've won but I was so stubborn, I refused to go down quietly. Like I said, I got lucky. Years later, I was cast with Woody in the 2017 film, *Wilson*, playing the scolding sister of his disenchanted ex-wife, Laura Dern. There was a scene in the dark comedy where Laura, who towers over me, got into a fistfight with me. Needless to say, she won. There was plenty of hair pulling, then she threw me across the kitchen counter and ended up pinning me to the floor and punched me in the nose. It was an intense scene but when we heard "cut" we'd hug each other and laugh.

In *The Grand*, I was married to Ray Romano. Ray had to leave before the end of filming because he had a family obligation, so we shot two final scenes before he left; one in which I won, and one in which I lost. At that point, we didn't know who would win the tournament, so we needed both options. We exchanged numbers because he wanted me to text him and let him know how the film ended. I was too shy to text him, though. I didn't want to disturb his time with his family.

At the wrap party, my friend Matt came up to me and said, "Can I pitch you a story for *Curb Your Enthusiasm?*"

"I'm not the person to pitch," I said, but he insisted.

So we stepped aside, and he launched into a story about trying to get his wife pregnant. He explained how he had to go to a fertility clinic, but he found the task of extracting a sperm sample challenging. The clinic had provided neither lube nor any good porn. At some point, I looked down and realized I had accidentally pocket-dialed Ray. My phone had called him multiple times while Matt was telling me this very personal, very detailed story.

I panicked. Ray was on the East Coast, and it was 3:00 in the morning for him. I was thinking, *Oh my god, he's married, with his family, and I've called him over and over in the middle of the night as I was having a conversation about sperm and lube. Who knows what he would think?* I started spiraling.

I asked a friend at the party what to do. Do I call and leave a message?

"Just stop. Don't do anything. Maybe he didn't even know it was you," she said.

I tried to calm down.

The next morning, Ray called me. "Did you call me four times last night?"

I started spiraling again. "Yes. Because Matt was telling me this crazy story about a fertility clinic, and he wasn't allowed to use lube, and they didn't have the kind of porn he liked, and I looked down and realized my phone had called you. Did you hear any of that?" I asked.

Unscripted

"No, but can you start over? And this time, talk slower," he said.

Ray has always had impeccable timing.

My love for poker got me invited to Costa Rica for another televised poker tournament. They flew me out there to play with a mix of pros and celebrities. Before the tournament started, we all got to know each other, and we made a deal: whoever won would split the prize of $50,000. First place would get $35,000, second place would get $10,000, and third place would get $5,000. It was winner-takes-all otherwise, so we figured at least three of us would walk away with something. Everyone agreed, except one poker pro.

"Nope. If it's winner-takes-all, it's winner-takes-all," he said.

We respected that. He wasn't soft, he was there to win. In the end, it didn't really matter because he didn't come in first, second or third. I walked away with $35K.

While I was there, I went to a dedication of a new playground at a local school. I was inspired by how much it meant to those kids. When I got back to LA, I told Paul I wanted to make a donation, in some way, to a school, but I didn't even know where to begin. He advised me to find a school in LA that could use some help.

At the time, I was volunteering with a program called Read Across America, reading to kids at an elementary school in Compton. So I cold-called the principal and told her I wanted to help by maybe providing the school with jump ropes or soccer balls. She invited me back to the school to show me around. That principal was Dr. Jacqueline Sanderlin. She's a force of nature.

We really hit it off. Her school was in rough shape. They only had two deflated soccer balls, no pump and no other equipment. We decided to work on the school together. Our goal was to raise enough money to put in a new playground for her scholars, as she called her students.

We decided to plan a fundraiser at the Groundlings. Larry David, Sarah Silverman, Rachael Harris, Kristin Wiig, and many other talented friends got involved. People were willing to pay a considerable amount of money to come watch us read scenes from old TV shows. There was something hilarious about watching them as the cast of *The Facts of Life*, *Baywatch*, and Larry as Uncle Jessie from *Full House*. It was a crowd pleaser, and I was beyond grateful to everyone who showed up to help. We raised money and started building a playground.

It didn't come without complications. I quickly learned the inner workings of school boards and how difficult it is to get approval for any kind of change. Thankfully, they worked with us. Jackie and I invited the community to get involved as well. Unsure if anyone would show up when the day came to work on the school, we almost cried when we saw a line of volunteers around the block. We painted the school, cleaned it up, planted flowers, and built that new playground. It definitely brought life back to the school. We all found joy watching the students on their landscaped playing field. The community surrounded the vibrant school, and the families stayed involved. Jackie told me property values around the school even went up. The whole experience filled my soul with happiness.

The next thing I knew, I was getting a call from Jackie. The school board wanted to move her to another school in hopes of her willingness to transform it. She asked if I'd work with her again, so we teamed up once more. Paul loved what we were doing and thought it should be a TV show that could demonstrate how communities can change their schools.

We pitched the idea to NBC, they said yes, and *School Pride* was created. We wanted our first on-camera school transformation to be in Compton because we knew the community was very strong and supportive. Most importantly, we knew we could rely on them for a good volunteer turnout. They did not disappoint.

When we wrapped at that school, we moved on to five more across the country including Kingston Springs, Tennessee; Baton Rouge, Louisiana; and Detroit, Michigan. When we were in Detroit, assessing a school, I asked a teacher why she put the trash can in the middle of the classroom. She told me that there was a leak in the roof. When it rained, water came streaming down through the ceiling tiles, so they needed it there to catch the water.

Many public schools across America have been overlooked and underserved. We found bathrooms that didn't work, fire alarms that were broken, and a shortage of school supplies that left teachers spending their own money on basics like pencils and paper. (That was over fifteen years ago, and unfortunately, there have not been significant changes in public schools since.) I butted heads with the other executive producer on *School Pride*. She made it clear we were to only make over the classrooms that were going to be on camera. I wanted every classroom in the schools to get some kind of upgrade, even if it was just a good cleaning and a new paint job.

I understood her stance because we had time and budget constraints, but it was upsetting when she told me I could work on the other classrooms, but not with any of the volunteers for the show. I wasn't allowed to use any of the show's resources. So, of course I depended on my family and friends to help. Chris, Mike, Becky, Paul Beckett, Eddie, Maria, Sarah, and even my assistant, Sarita volunteered. They scrubbed, vacuumed, bought paint and painting supplies, and organized our own rag tag volunteer team to give every school a makeover. The teachers, students, and parents all helped. Mike refloored a gymnasium practically by himself. Jackie and I were very proud of all we accomplished.

Years later, when I found out I was receiving a star on the Hollywood Walk of Fame, I was shocked. Warner Brothers had graciously nominated me. They were the studio behind my new sitcom *Suburgatory*, and the committee wanted to recognize both my on-camera work and my community contributions in Los Angeles. It was truly a high point in my career. My entire family, including little Michael, was there. My agent leaned over to me at the time and said, "That's your sitcom right there."

She pointed to the front row where my TV husband, Larry David; my future husband, Bobby Kennedy Jr.; and my ex-husband, Paul Young, sat side by side.

***

I've been fortunate to have had the funniest and most talented on-screen husbands. Larry was my first TV husband and Robin Williams was my first film husband. In 2005, I was cast in the family comedy film *RV*. In lieu of an audition, I met with the director Barry Sonnenfeld. He was hilarious and neurotic, which is right up my alley. That first meeting with him was easily the most fun interview I've ever had. Toward the end of our discussion, he asked me who I thought was more neurotic—him or Larry. I wasn't sure where he was going with the question, and I wasn't sure where I was going with my answer. It's in my nature to always be honest.

"Well, this is really hard. I know Larry better, so I can see a side of him that's a little less neurotic, but from the little time we've had together, I might have to say it's you. I mean, you're full-court press neurotic."

I got the part.

When I walked in for the table read, I paused for just a moment to take it all in. There was a long conference table set up for us at Sony Studios with microphones and small cameras perched in front of each actor's spot. I could see my name place setting next to Robin Williams's with Jeff Daniels's on the other side of me. I felt like I was dreaming.

Robin, whom I'd never met, walked right up to me and hugged me. It was a true, authentic hug. He made me feel like we'd been friends forever. "You're in the movies now, kid," he whispered in my ear. He was reading my mind. Jeff was equally as gracious, putting me at ease before the high-pressure table read. I knew we were going to have a great time. And I was right.

We shot the film in Canada and we were all on the road together for three or four months. Cat wasn't yet two, so I brought her along with me. There's a flashback scene in the film where I'm holding my baby. Barry suggested we use Cat, so she made her film debut as a baby Josh Hutcherson. To this day she questions our decision to cast her as a boy in her first big screen appearance. She was perfect though. I held her while we watched Robin do a puppet show for the young version of JoJo, our daughter in the film. Every day was a little adventure with Barry, Robin, Josh, and JoJo. Naturally, we spent a lot of time together in an RV. Barry is an iconoclast. He loves cowboys and he directed the film from a Western saddle mounted on an apple box. He has never been on a real horse. He sported a magnificent (fake) country moustache during filming, put in place by the makeup crew each morning. I loved every second I spent with them.

We shot one scene in which Robin was at the wheel and the rest of us were listening to our own music with our headphones on. Robin's purpose for the trip was solace and family time. His expectations reached a fever pitch as he found himself the lonely driver, while his family, each with their own headphones on, were singing along to different songs at the top of our lungs. When it came time for me to record the audio for my song, "G.T.O." by Ronny & The Daytonas, Barry and the sound crew joined me in one of the RVs. Barry suggested I try singing straightforwardly with no attempt at humor. He thought he could give me direction to find the comedy in it later.

"Okay," I told Barry, who was sitting inches away from me in an adjacent seat. "I'm not a great singer, but I'll do my best."

"Just do your best," he reassured me.

I had my headphones on, and my eyes closed tight in concentration. No one could hear the song but me.

I sang both the lead and back-up vocals to the best of my ability. I didn't hold back. I wanted Barry to know what our starting baseline would be so he could give me notes on how I could improve my next take.

When the song was over, I opened my eyes only to see Barry laughing uproariously with tears streaming down his face. He assured me he had exactly what he needed. There would be no need for a second take. I walked onto the set the next day and I could see the crew listening to something and laughing their asses off. Barry had sent my a cappella recording of "G.T.O." to all of them for their listening pleasure.

I have a collection of little intimate moments from different shoots that I carry with me in a mental scrapbook. I like to flip through it when I hear an actor's name I've worked with or just need a ray of light when I'm feeling downhearted. I have many pages devoted to Robin.

Robin was an extraordinarily sweet soul as well as a groundbreaking comedic voice. Out of his mind came unending lightning bolts of genius and a thousand separate characters, easily rendered with his perfect ear for accent and expression. Each of them was consciously rooted in his ability to access his own pain as he delivered Oscar-worthy dramatic performances. He couldn't help himself from doing comedy bits when they came to him—even in the lunch line during our shooting breaks. If he had an audience of only one, he'd still hit the joke like he was filming one of his HBO comedy specials. On a particularly hot day, I made the mistake of confiding in Robin that I was worried my deodorant was giving out and apologized if I was stinky. He immediately lifted my arm, stuck his nose deep into my armpit and acted like he was breathing in a summer breeze in the middle of a rose garden. I was wearing a sleeveless top.

My mom came to Canada to help me take care of Cat, and every time she visited the set, he'd walk over to her, call her by name and give her a hug. She could never get over the fact that Robin Williams knew her name. He must've known how much that simple gesture would mean to her. While he was preparing for his next scene, his next stunt, his next monologue, he made it a priority to say hello to my mom. He was the best of the best.

Chapter 9

The journey to the monumental moment of getting a star cemented on Hollywood Boulevard was filled with twists and turns. I was navigating the murky waters of show business the best I could. I had always heard about the proverbial "casting couch" but only had one incident that floated into that territory. While I was still working as an assistant, I was approached by a man at a drugstore in Beverly Hills. He said I looked like I could be an actress. I confirmed that I was. He introduced himself as James Toback, a writer and director. He listed some of the films he had made, including penning the Oscar nominated script for *Bugsy*. I was familiar with his films.

I didn't get any kind of sense that he was being inappropriate. He looked like he was twenty years older than me. He told me he was working on a new film and would like to discuss a part for which he considered me perfect. He was only going to be in town for a few days and asked me to meet him at the Beverly Hills Hotel on Friday night. I called my agent after our exchange. I asked if it seemed like a bad idea to meet him at a hotel. He told me he thought it was fine. This director was legitimate, he said, and it wasn't that uncommon for an out-of-town filmmaker to take meetings in their hotel suites. He encouraged me to go.

My sixth sense was registering a mild concern, so I brought back-up. A group of friends from the Groundlings agreed to meet me in the hotel bar, and as I left them for the meeting, I gave them the room number and said, "Okay, if you don't hear from me in thirty minutes, come to this room."

When he answered my knock, I told Mr. Toback that I had friends waiting for me downstairs. Just like my agent had said, it was a hotel suite, and we took our seats in his living room. Toback was engaging and interesting. He explained that his new film involved a college student on an LSD trip. He asked about my approach to acting and if I am able to move outside of my comfort zone, to which I answered yes. I got my first red flag. He asked me if I had a lot of body hair.

"Body hair?" I asked, looking at the peach fuzz on my arm. "No, not really."

He suggested I take my boots off to get more comfortable.

"No, that's okay. I'm comfortable," I said.

Then he suggested I take off just one boot.

"What? One boot? Why would I take off one boot?" I asked.

He reiterated the idea of being able to step out of my comfort zone. I don't know why, but I found the suggestion mildly amusing. I was curious to know what was going on. Why one boot? I took off one boot and left my sock on. We continued on with our conversation until it was interrupted with a loud knock at the door.

"That must be my friends," I said as I sprang up to answer the door.

I opened the door and there they all were, like a sitcom where everyone's head is crammed in the doorway. One of my friends said, "Cheryl, where's your boot?"

"Oh, it's over there," I pointed.

"Get your boot and let's go," he said. "Why do you only have one boot on?"

"Yeah, it *is* weird, isn't it?" I asked.

I grabbed my boot and rushed out the door, pulling it on as I bolted hurriedly down the hallway. I never heard from that director again.

That was in 2000. Then in 2017, during the #MeToo movement, I started to hear a great deal about him—James Toback had been accused of sexual misconduct and sexual abuse by hundreds of women, including high profile actresses like Selma Blair and Rachel McAdams. Many of the women's stories had similar initiations to mine, but turned dark as they were trapped alone with Toback. He would manipulate young women into undressing incrementally under the guise of an audition and then sexually assault them. Apparently, one common theme was that he would rub himself against their leg and ejaculate. Some forty women filed a lawsuit against him in New York, winning $1.68 billion dollars in damages.

Thankfully, that night didn't escalate for me. But reading others' accounts later, I understood how quickly things could have gone south. It wasn't until years later, when I read Gavin de Becker's book, *The Gift of Fear*, that I started to understand how well-meaning women and men can get drawn into a dangerous predator's web of premeditated sexual abuse and violence.

Chapter 10

It took a *Seinfeld* reunion to get back into Larry's TV life again. Although I was still on *Curb*, my role had become less prominent as Larry's ex-wife. In Season 7, Larry decided to orchestrate a *Seinfeld* reunion as a storyline on *Curb*. There had been talk of a real *Seinfeld* show reunion, but it never materialized.

According to the plotline, Larry masterminded this reunion so he could cast my character, Cheryl David, plotting to win her back. He knew it would mean a lot to her. Working with him would surely cause me to fall in love with him again.

Warner Brothers reconstructed the original set on a soundstage, and it was absolutely surreal standing in Jerry's apartment and sitting in the booth at Monk's Café, shooting scenes with the cast of the iconic show. Within the *Curb* storyline, Jerry and Jason are skeptical about Larry's choice to cast Cheryl David in the role of George's ex-wife. They pitched a lineup of more established actresses: Meg Ryan, Jennifer Tilly, Kristin Chenoweth, or Lisa Kudrow. But Larry—preoccupied with his romance fantasy—contrived a parade of unconvincing reasons for rejecting each of them.

Larry lamely tried to convince them that I alone was perfect for the part. It would be advantageous, he argued, to cast an unknown actress, just like he had originally cast me on *Curb Your Enthusiasm* in 1999. Jerry insisted that I audition for the role.

That scene turned into the most nerve-wracking moment I'd had shooting *Curb*. In the show, I auditioned for Larry and Jerry, reading with Marc Hirschfeld, the actual Emmy-nominated casting director of *Seinfeld*. It was art imitating art imitating life! Because *Curb* was improvised, we never had scripts, but when it came time to shoot the scene, they gave me a script to read during the audition.

"You want me to cold-read this on camera? During the scene? I mean, Cheryl David is auditioning for the *Seinfeld* reunion. Can I have a minute with the script to look at my lines?" I asked.

Larry assured me that I needn't worry about pre-reading the script. "You're going to get the part! You're overthinking this."

In the end, Larry stormed off the *Seinfeld* set because he suspected Jason was making a move on me. In an unusual turn on *Curb*, Larry and I had a romantic scene together when I appeared unannounced at his place to watch the "Seinfeld Reunion" with him. I told him I had also quit the show because it just wasn't the same without him there. We happily watched Elisabeth Shue play the role of George's ex-wife, and he turned to me and said, ". . . That ending was better than the one I wrote, I have to say."

"It was, yeah. Because they belong together," I said.

"Really?" he asked.

"Don't you think?" I replied.

"Are you sure?"

"I'm absolutely positive," I said as we leaned in for a reconciliatory kiss.

Unscripted

Just as things were working out the way he hoped, he noticed the water ring my iced coffee was leaving on his table. In an earlier episode, Julia had accused him of leaving a ring stain on her antique table. No matter how much he assured her he "respected wood," she couldn't move away from the idea that he was the culprit.

"Do you respect wood?" he asked me.

"I guess so," I said as I leaned in to continue our long-awaited kiss.

Unable to let it go, he asked, "You guess so? You don't know if you respect wood?"

"I've never thought about it before. I guess I do," I said.

The conversation quickly devolved into an argument. He insisted I call Julia and tell her I was guilty of the water stain on her table, but I refused to do it. And just like that, the possibility of a reconciliation went up in smoke. Cue the *Curb* theme.

Chapter 11

I first met Bobby Kennedy Jr. at a Waterkeeper pro/celebrity ski fundraising event in 2005. I had accompanied Larry to attend a charity dinner in Banff, Canada. Bobby had been close friends with Larry since the *Seinfeld* days, and their families spent summers together on Cape Cod.

Neither Larry nor I had any intention of skiing at this event, but when we ran into Bobby, he immediately started fitting us in boots and skis. The next thing I knew, the three of us and Ed Begley Jr. were on a frozen chairlift in the subzero Canadian cold. Bobby noticed I was cold, and handed me his wool cap, which prompted Larry to remind us that he was bald and needed his hat, but if he had a headful of hair, he would've gladly given his up. Bobby struck me as kind and polite, but I didn't think much of it.

It was six years later when I ran into Bobby at another Waterkeeper event that my life took a 180-degree turn. I was now separated, living on my own as a single mom while I waited for my divorce to be finalized. Bobby had filed for divorce a year earlier, and this encounter was a completely different experience. It was the first time Bobby and I really talked, really got to know each other.

I was there with my brother Mike, my nephew Graham, and my friend Maria. Bobby and I had known each other for a few years, always friendly, but that night, I felt as if I was seeing him for the first time. We were both newly single. I'd only been on one uneventful date with a well-meaning, determined, much younger guy I had met while helping Cat sell Girl Scout cookies. The other moms there begged me to go out with him so they could live vicariously through me. They were highly disappointed when I recapped our small talk at dinner and early evening.

This felt like the first time I truly *saw* Bobby. He pulled me aside and spoke quietly, "Sit next to me at dinner."

It seems cliché, but I was thunderstruck from the moment we started talking. It felt like I was seeing his face for the first time. I don't know how I missed before how blue his eyes are. I felt his magnetic energy. There were so many things I hadn't noticed before. The instantaneous electric connection swept me along. He has since told me he felt the same way. He thought I looked different that night for some reason too.

As the night went on, Bobby regaled us with stories from his life: how he had spent a summer in a maximum security prison in Puerto Rico when he was suing the US Navy to stop its live-fire exercises at Camp Garcia on Vieques. He recounted that his family had a pet seal when he was growing up who loved to eat fish but would spit out the eyeballs. He even told some long jokes with a questionable Irish brogue. He was an expert ski racer, a master falconer, an avid fisherman, and champion equestrian. He had written books on the environment, history, politics, and St. Francis of Assisi. I was smitten. Maria witnessed the whole thing.

"He just looked at you like he wanted to devour your soul," she whispered to me with a mixture of mischief and delight.

My brother Mike was also taken with Bobby. "He's quite the Renaissance man. Seems like he can do anything. If he walked into a room and saw a piccolo in the corner, I wouldn't be surprised if he just strolled over and started playing it."

We had a great time together skiing and mixing with the celebrity guests and some legendary ski racers. I dreaded saying good-bye to Bobby.

I returned to Los Angeles on cloud nine. I felt like I had met a creature from another universe. He was living in a world completely unfamiliar to mine. He was a prominent environmental attorney fighting injustices for people who had no voice. He traveled around the globe with kings and lived in the wilderness with Indian tribes. Nothing about him was ordinary, except maybe his pleated khakis. I couldn't wait to see him again.

We skied together in Aspen a few weeks later over Christmas and I got to spend time with his children, and again when we both attended the Sundance Film Festival. He was there to promote a documentary on mountaintop removal miners. I was there for a Creative Coalition event. We hung out between events and film screenings. It was a whirlwind. I wanted more time with him to figure out who he was. I was captivated by his charisma and intellect. I was moved by how light and joyful he'd seemed even though I knew he had experienced a parade of loss and sorrow. Everything about him felt one shade deeper and a degree more intense than anyone I'd ever met—spiritually, intellectually, romantically.

We took advantage of every occasion to be together, especially when work travel landed us in the same time zone. I was in NYC doing press for *Curb Your Enthusiasm,* when Bobby texted asking me to meet him at the 79th St. Boat Basin on the Hudson River at 5:00. He wanted to show me something. He was at work and didn't have time to give me more details. At least that's how I justified the cryptic note.

"What should I wear?" I typed.

"Doesn't matter. See you in a little while," he texted.

Doesn't matter? I hated *doesn't matter*. Since the words boat basin and pier were in the text, I decided to keep it casual with sensible flats. I showed up at 5:00 and watched him get out of his dilapidated minivan. He waved as he ran up to me and grabbed my hand.

"Come on, we've gotta go," he said.

We rushed along to the dock, climbed into a tiny zodiac dinghy that he pushed off the pier. My shoes got soaked immediately.

"Don't worry about that. You can take them off. You won't need them," he said.

"I won't need my shoes?" I asked.

"Push off on your side as hard as you can," he said.

We pushed the inflatable vessel away from the dock as Bobby maneuvered through the harbor. I was impressed. He had arranged to take me out on the river in a little boat.

"This is really sweet, Bobby. Thank you for bringing me here," I said.

"No, no. This isn't it," he laughed. "You think I wanted to show you a dinghy?"

"I have no idea. Why don't you just tell me what we're doing?" I asked.

About a hundred yards upriver, in a mooring field, we pulled up next to a proper boat, a twenty-eight-foot center console Mako called *Riverkeeper*. He quickly fastened the dinghy to the mooring.

Taking my hand, he said, "Come on. We've got to jump in." He helped me onto the boat.

Bobby cranked up the twin 250 horsepower engines, and we took off. We cruised up to the George Washington Bridge and then downriver past the *USS Intrepid* aircraft carrier. He pointed to the bluff on the New Jersey side where Aaron Burr had killed Alexander Hamilton in their famous duel and showed me a view of Manhattan and the Battery most people never see. We soon approached the Statue of Liberty.

"This is what I wanted you to see. Isn't she beautiful?" He asked.

The setting sun cloaked the statue in a luminous orange glow. She was much grander and larger than I had imagined. My heart was on overload. I looked at Bobby, his blue eyes sparkling, as he smiled at me.

"Wow. I can't believe this!" I said. "Yes, she's very beautiful."

At that moment, the rest of the world seemed to melt away. The only thing I could see was the water, the sunset, the Statue of Liberty and Bobby. I closed my eyes for a minute and made myself burn the image into my memory.

The river was crowded with ferries, tugboats pushing cement and oil barges, and lots of boats similar to Bobby's. He told me that it didn't look like this a decade earlier when the river was polluted and New York had turned its back on the Hudson.

He had spent decades fighting against industrial and municipal pollution in the river. He used his leadership and lawyering skills to build his environmental advocacy organization, Riverkeeper, and worked with the NRDC, (the Natural Resources Defense Council) to enforce the Clean Water Act and other environmental laws. He successfully sued the river's biggest polluters, including dozens of sewer plants, Exxon Mobil, and General Electric that had dumped millions of pounds of toxic PCBs, or polychlorinated biphenyls, into the river. He had forced GE to dredge contaminated sediment and remove the toxic pollution from the river. It was hard to imagine what the river must've been like then. I could only see a vibrant, bustling waterway.

I studied Bobby as he recounted for me the biological and human history of the Hudson and the fight that transformed the river from an open sewer to the global model for ecosystem protection. It seemed that the tragedies and struggles he had endured and those combative years in court had etched indelible lines into his handsome face. I started to understand Bobby's passion for the Hudson and why he wanted to share the river with me.

We headed back to the dock before we lost daylight. I put my wet shoes back on as I got out of the dinghy. Bobby and I walked down the dock, hand in hand as the sun disappeared. We got into his car, and I was still floating in a dreamlike haze. I would've sworn I was dreaming, but my feet were cold and the rancid smell of roadkill in Bobby's minivan was enough to know all of it was real.

**

I met Bobby's mother, Ethel, the first weekend I stayed with him in Hyannis Port. A lot of people refer to it as the Kennedy Compound but those closest to it don't usually call it that. They just refer to it as *The Cape*. This historical spot includes several adjacent nineteenth-century white clapboard houses that have been in the family for generations, clustered together along the shores of Nantucket Sound and surrounded by perfectly manicured green grass framed by gardens of giant light blue hydrangeas. Many of the homes have widows' walks or railed rooftop platforms where sailors' wives once watched for their husbands to return from the sea.

When John F. Kennedy was president, his Hyannis Port home was the Summer White House. Just inside the sawgrass buffer, a sprawling grassy field served as a weekend landing pad for presidential helicopters that brought the president, Bobby's father Attorney General Robert F. Kennedy, and several uncles who also served in the White House to the Cape each weekend during those three summers of his presidency. They included Peace Corps Director Sargent Shriver, White House Chief of Staff Stephen Smith, and Senator Edward Kennedy.

Framed photos on every wall and table document the Camelot era. Jack and Jackie, their kids, Sargent and Eunice, Teddy and Joan, Stephen and Jean, Robert Kennedy and Ethel, and dozens of children, sailing, waterskiing, riding horses, and playing football and baseball on the iconic lawns.

There was a birthday party for one of Bobby's cousins that weekend. I was seated next to Ethel, under a giant white tent packed with family and friends, dressed in khakis, jeans, blue blazers and summer dresses, all there to give toasts, (or more like roasts) complete with friendly heckling and jibing, which grew especially raucous when one of the Shrivers had the floor. In the endearing blockback from generations of friendly interfamily competing, I saw both the warmth and the rivalry. I had an immediate bond with Ethel, who made me laugh with her witty and irreverent off-the-cuff commentary. Leaning over, she asked if everything was as I expected.

I had to think for a moment.

"Well, honestly, I don't think I had any expectations. I never imagined what it would be like here," I said candidly. "But now that you ask, I'm surprised at how warm and welcoming everyone has been."

"Really?" She asked. "I'm glad to hear that."

"Your family reminds me of mine. It's much bigger, but we're very close and we just love being with each other."

Ethel and I chatted the whole night. She was funny, direct, and perfectly happy to tell me what she liked and didn't like, with equal vigor.

The next day as I explored the tiny seaside village, I kept thinking about her question. Maybe I was expecting more formality there. I guess I didn't think Ethel would be found barefoot, even at dinner. She was always perfectly put together in her summer outfits, but shoeless. Her house was beautiful, understated, and unpretentious. The refrigerator was a 1970s vintage, but why not? It worked properly. Like most people's, her house was adorned with family photos, but her sixties-era black and white photos of presidents, kings, and popes made it more like a relaxed and comfortable museum. They were intimate portraits documenting one of the high points in American history.

As I spent more time there, I learned the lay of the land. The summers were filled with boat rides, cookouts, and lots of games ranging from volleyball, softball, and capture the flag—running across five yards—to running charades in the living room. It's a very competitive group. Even the indoor games could be physically hazardous. My friend, Gail, ended up in the emergency room one night when she twisted her ankle running up the stairs to get her next clue. Our house was always packed with kids and teenagers. We only have a few bathrooms in the house, so when everyone is getting ready at the same time to go to a dinner party, it was complete mayhem. When my friend, Suzanne, came to visit, she learned to shower in her bathing suit after a series of upsetting interruptions. A complete stranger could decide to use the bathroom at any given moment.

I adored Ethel. She was the matriarch of this big, loud family of loving, but unruly children who understood that the only rules they could never break were Ethel's.

Any family members who happened to be staying for the summer, were always welcome to her place for cocktails at five. Everyone understood that you show up nicely dressed. Dinner was at six, but she insisted that you arrange to have a spot at the table ahead of time. It was a sit-down dinner and required a lot of preparation so last-minute additions were discouraged. Otherwise, she would've been squeezing forty people in at her table every night. Ethel was relaxed about many things, but when it came to table manners, she expected perfection.

The first time I joined her and the crew for dinner, Bobby suggested I sit next to Ethel, which I did happily. It didn't take long to realize that I was in the hot seat. Bobby and one of his brothers sat at the opposite side of the long dining table, and one of them told a racy joke at a volume that they knew Ethel wouldn't quite be able to hear. Their loud laughter provoked Ethel to ask me to repeat it to her. The table couldn't wait to hear what I was going to say.

"What did he say?" Ethel asked me.

"Oh, he said something about a shepherd being lonely out in the middle of nowhere, with only his sheep to keep him company," I said.

"Well, that's not funny. There must be more to it, everyone's laughing," she said.

"Oh, right. Well, he would watch some of the other shepherds with their sheep . . . something, something, something . . ." I said, hoping to skip to the end of the joke.

"Don't say, something, something, something. He didn't say something, something, something. Just repeat what he said," she insisted.

"Okay. He'd watch the other guys have . . . inappropriate relations with the sheep . . ." I said.

She turned to the person on her right and gestured toward me, "What is she saying? Do you know what she's saying?"

Everyone at the table was enjoying this translation game. She turned back to me.

"What does inappropriate relations mean?" she asked.

"Well, I'm repeating what they said, but I'm guessing they're talking about the shepherd having a physical relationship with a sheep," I said uneasily.

Her face lit up with shock and disgust.

"I don't know what you're trying to do here, but this isn't something you should be discussing at the dinner table or at all for that matter," she scolded me.

"Of course not, I completely agree with you. Your sons were the ones telling this joke," I reminded her.

"I'd hardly call it a joke," she said. "Is that it? That's not funny."

"No, there's a little more to it," I said hesitantly.

She looked at her neighbor again. "What's wrong with her? Why is she taking so long?" Then she turned back to me, "Come on. We don't have all night."

"Right, okay, anyway, the shepherd was so lonely, he finally decided to engage in an inappropriate, romantic act with one of his sheep . . ."

"Oh!" she interjected disapprovingly.

"And then one of the other shepherds laughed at him. He said, why are you laughing? Because you picked an ugly one," I said.

That caused an outburst at the table. Bobby's siblings and friends acted wildly offended.

"Cheryl!" One would say.

"I can't believe you're saying this," another would say.

Ethel locked eyes with me and said, "Now why would you tell a joke like that at the table?"

"It wasn't actually my joke, I was just repeating it," I said, defending myself.

She looked at the rest of the table, surprised by my brashness.

"Who would say something like that at dinner?" she'd ask.

This would rouse another round of: "Cheryl!"

"I can't believe you're talking like this in front of our mother!"

"Why would you tell a joke like that at the table?"

The laughter filled the house as we finished dinner. Ethel's comedic timing was impeccable as she told anecdotes from her extraordinary life. I can't help but to think she knew her part in the translation game and played it perfectly. This sort of thing would continue all summer. It was a high price to pay to sit next to Ethel, but it was well worth it.

***

When Bobby and I were still dating, we took a trip to Cuba for a scuba diving expedition with The Explorers Club, which was conducting a reef survey in the Gardens of the Queen, one of the world's largest marine parks. We had Cat and Bobby's sons, Aidan and Conor, with us. Bobby hoped to reconnect with Castro, but we hadn't received a confirmation, so we assumed the meeting wasn't going to happen. When we arrived at our hotel in Havana, a guy in a white linen suit and a Panama hat was waiting for us in the lobby. Shaking Bobby's hand, he said, "El Presidente will see you tomorrow."

He told us that only our family members could attend, and we should not bring phones or cameras. He would return to collect us in the morning.

We went out to explore Havana. We visited Ernest Hemingway's favorite bar, El Floridita, where the daiquiri was invented, and we marveled at all the 1950s American cars. We strode through a plaza where recently relaxed rules that prohibited private business were allowing capitalism to make its first inroads in Cuba since the Revolution. There were some cigar vendors and ladies plaiting hair for the tourists. Cat wanted to get her hair braided. As I stood by waiting, the women persuaded me to get mine braided too. I said no, but when I sat down in a chair to wait, they just started braiding my hair anyway. I kept saying, "I really don't want this," but they persisted.

When Bobby returned, the woman said to him in Spanish, "You owe us seventy dollars."

"Seventy dollars for what?" he asked, speaking Spanish as well.

"We just braided their hair," she said.

He glanced over to see my head covered with small, tight braids. It couldn't have looked good. Bobby confirmed my suspicions.

"You look like a crazy person," he laughed.

"I know! I didn't even want this!" I said as I started pulling the braids out.

"That seems like a lot," he continued to the woman in Spanish. "You're charging for hers, too? She said she didn't even want them."

"Well, that's how much it is. I'll just call the police," she threatened.

"Okay, let's call the police," he said.

They motioned for a nearby policewoman to come over. Bobby explained what happened.

"Okay, you all need to come with me," she said.

Bobby translated everything to Cat and me as we walked toward the courthouse. She took us to a building that looked like a medieval Spanish fort, leading us over a moat on a drawbridge.

When we got to the foreboding building, the police said only Cat, the woman and I could go in.

I insisted on Bobby coming with us so he could translate. "I don't speak Spanish, I'm not going to be helpful."

Inside, Bobby's explaining everything to the judge in Spanish. I'm catching bits and pieces. Every now and then, he'd point to me and say, "*Muy feo.*" Which means "very ugly."

"How dare you!" I told him, before quietly conceding. "Okay, I get it. I can't pull off the tiny braid look. I know."

Eventually, the judge rendered his verdict. "This is a ridiculous amount of money. Don't pay her anything. She was trying to take advantage of you."

Turning to the vendor, he explained the rules of competition: "If you order food in a restaurant,"—at that time, there were only three or four restaurants in Havana—"if you don't like it, you don't have to pay—the same is true here."

Bobby insisted on paying the woman for braiding Cat's hair, which looked adorable, by the way, but the judge wasn't having it.

The next day, when we went to see Castro, Cat still had her braids in. Despite my protests, she demanded that she wear her T-shirt that said, "Smile, Pass it on." We sat in Castro's living room listening, as "El Presidente" and Bobby conversed in Spanish. A translator worked to include Cat, Aidan, Conor, and me in the conversation. Bobby and Castro talked for hours. They spoke about unsuccessful assassination attempts orchestrated by the US on Castro's life. Bobby and Castro agreed his father and uncle were never involved. They spoke about how the CIA sent Castro a wetsuit as a "gift" from an emissary that RFK sent to Cuba to negotiate a prisoner exchange for the Bay of Pigs POWs. The emissary, who Bobby knew, had no idea that the agency had put poison in the wetsuit. Castro talked to the children about the miracle of the internet and a wide range of other issues ranging from his friendship with Jacques Cousteau (he told them that it was Cousteau who convinced him to protect Gardens of the Queen) to the perils of space junk. He delighted the children with his very detailed answers to their questions about Batista, his guerrilla campaign in the Sierra Maestras, his flight from Mexico on the ship *Granma*, which they had seen the previous day in the National Museum, and his father's role as a soldier in the Cuban War of Independence. It was rather surreal to be sitting in Castro's living room, him in his matching blue tracksuit, calmly drinking homemade lemonade, listening to his vivid stories of Cuban history.

The next day, we were out in the middle of the ocean for our ten-day trip on the dive boat. We would take small boats out to each dive site to survey the coral reefs. On the third day, Bobby's boat returned before mine. When I pulled up, there was a large naval vessel tied up to our dive boat. One of the women from our group ran up to me and said, "I don't know how to tell you this, but the Cuban police are here. They're armed. They asked permission to board the boat. They're looking for Bobby."

"That sounds about right. Where are they now?" I asked.

I walked up to the front of the boat, bracing myself for what I might find, only to see Bobby, the police officers, and the boat captain smiling for pictures. Castro had printed out photos for us that his son had taken during our visit. Somehow, the police had tracked us down in the middle of the ocean to deliver them. He had sent each of the kids a picture with a handwritten note. His note to Cat complimented her on her braids and agreed no one should pay that much for a hair styling. Castro wrote: "Nobody has ever paid me that much even for a seven-hour speech. It's more than you would pay at a restaurant for the finest octopus in Seville."

Cheryl Hines

I still have the photo of Cat and Castro. It was just another day in the life with Bobby. Around this same time, my life took another hairpin turn I could've never anticipated.

Chapter 12

There's a famous line in Ernest Hemingway's *The Sun Also Rises*: "How did you go bankrupt?"

"Two ways. Gradually, and then suddenly."

My journey had been a slow, steady climb but with luck, forbearance, faith, and hard work, I had built the life of my dreams: a fulfilling acting career, a close-knit family, and friends that kept me endlessly entertained and loved all while being with a man who captured my heart and imagination. It had taken me twenty years to get here, but I felt completely content and grateful. In the span of a year, my life was about to take a series of life-changing turns. I wasn't going bankrupt, but my life changed with head-spinning speed.

By then, I had developed a special friendship with Bobby's sixteen-year-old daughter Kyra. Kyra was struggling in school, and Bobby asked if I would consider allowing her to live at my house while she attended school in Los Angeles. I loved Kyra and was happy to take her in. Suddenly, Cat had an older sister.

It started with a phone call from The Boys asking me to come to their apartment. Unlike the endless lighthearted banter that I was accustomed to, the tone was somber.

They sat me down and Paul told me he had a brain tumor behind his left ear and was going into surgery the following morning. He waited until the last minute to tell me because he didn't want me contacting his parents back in Tallahassee. He didn't want anyone to know.

"Don't you think your mom should know?" I asked. I was struggling to process what I was hearing.

"No. She'll want to fly out here. I don't want to worry her." he said sternly.

"At least call her," I said.

"No. This is why I waited to tell you. It's too late for her to fly out here. I'll tell her after the surgery, when it's all over. Don't even tell Becky. It's not a big deal," he insisted.

Paul's stubbornness was intractable. When he had his mind made up there was no changing it.

"Are you scared?" I asked.

I was, but something about the way he was talking—he seemed so clear and unperturbed—was starting to calm my fears.

"No. Not at all," he said, matter of factly. "It happens all the time. This is very common and it's nothing to worry about. That's why I didn't even want to tell you. I don't want you to worry. It'll be too stressful for me."

"I made him tell you," Eddie said.

"Thank you, Eddie," I replied. "Okay, I'm going to try my best not to worry."

"You can't," Eddie said, "or he'll be really mad at me."

Me in third grade

My dad, Jim, with Chris, Becky, and me

Me, Michael, Chris, and Becky

Me and my friends from chorus in High School—Molly, Linda, Tammy, and Lori

My high school friend Valerie, Chris, Mike, and me at Studebaker's in Tallahassee

Chris, Becky, me, and Mike

Me, my Grandmother Ruth, and Becky

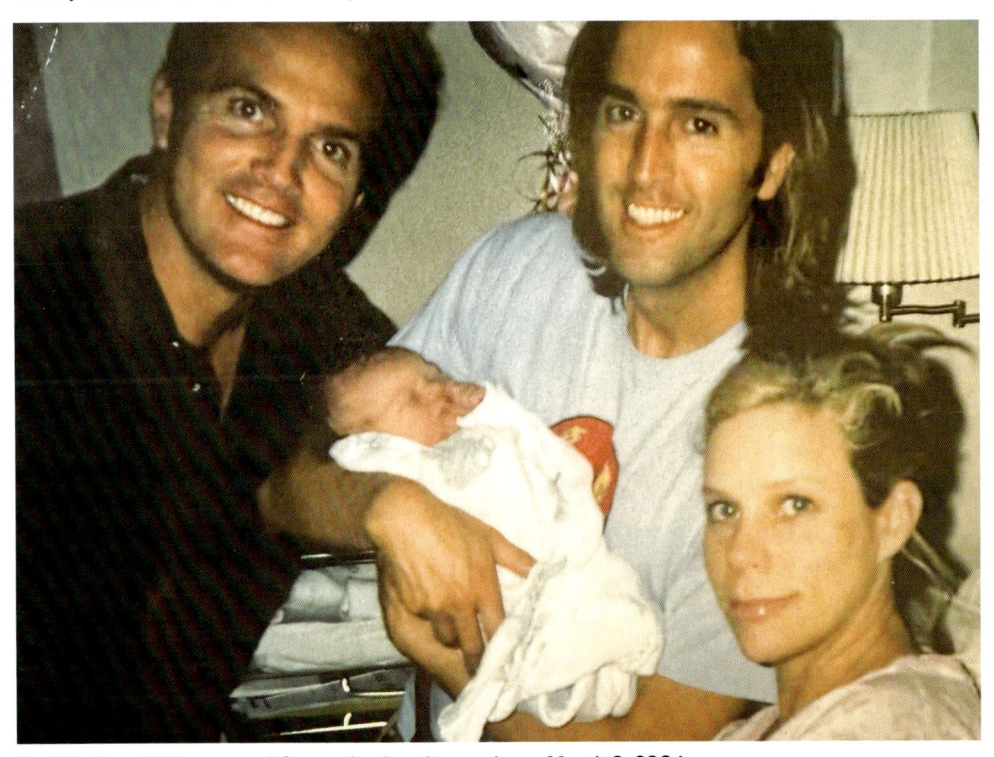

Paul Beckett, Eddie, me, and Cat on the day she was born, March 8, 2004

From *Psycho* Universal Studios days

My mom, me, and Cat in my trailer while shooting *RV*

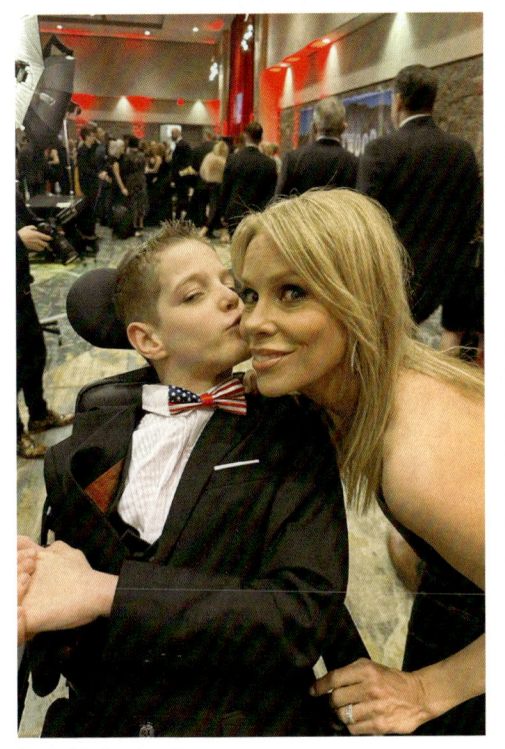

Little Michael and me

Little Michael

Me cleaning my star on the Hollywood Walk of Fame

Cracklin' Rosie (my mom) and me

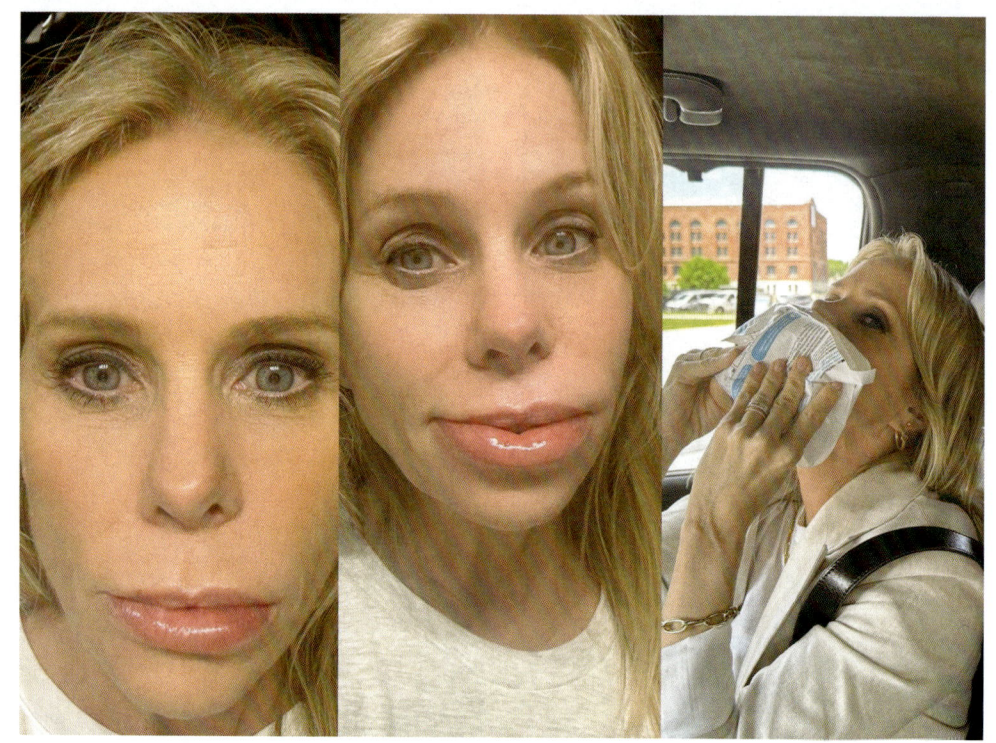

Me in Milwaukee (2024) when I broke into hives and my lower lip swelled due to stress

Me, Cat, and Paul Young (Cat's dad, my ex-husband)

Robin Williams, me, and Barry Sonnenfeld at the *RV* premiere

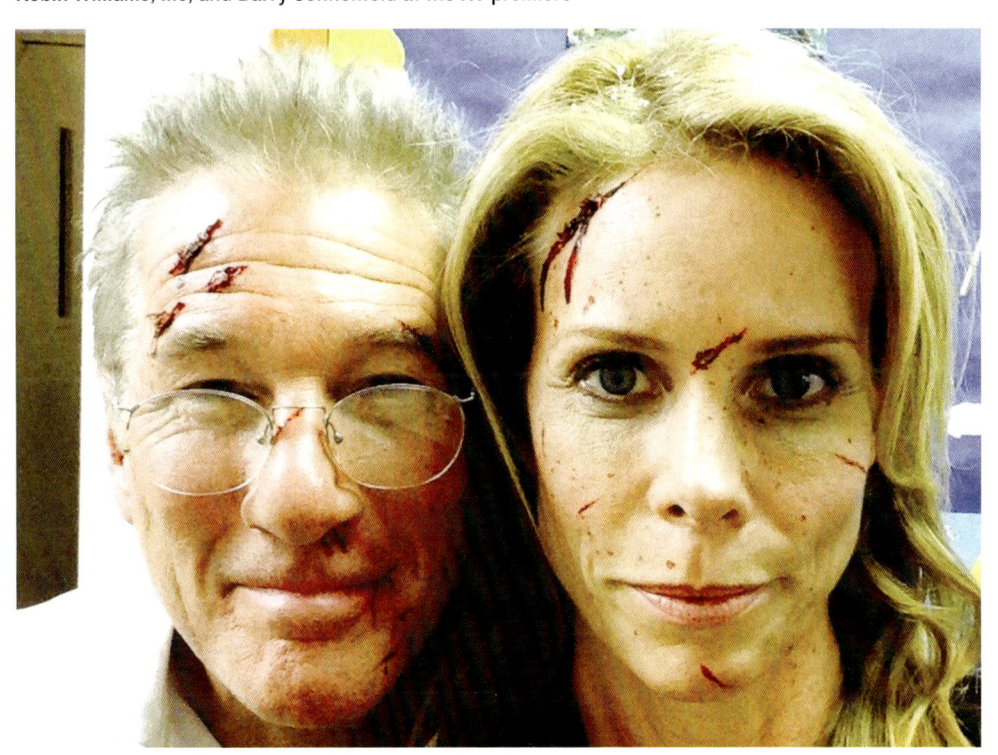

Richard Gere and me

Me and Toby

Ronan and me

Bobby and Little Michael at Gatorland

Toby in the house in Malibu

Right after we said "I Do"

Bobby, me, and Larry at our wedding

Bobby and me and the family at our wedding

Cassius, Bobby III, Kick, Aidan, Amaryllis, BobCat, Bobby, me, Kyra, and Finn

Ethel at her table set with the proper glasses at our wedding

Bobby, Cat, Cate, Zoe, me, Little Michael, Mike, Chris, and Jackson in 2015 at Washington Nationals' spring training game

(above and below) Bobby and me

Becky, Chris, me, Cat, Phil (stepdad), Mike, and my mom after filming *Celebrity Family Feud* (We won!)

Kick, Amaryllis, Zoe, Bobby III, Conor, Finn, Cat, Bobby, Kyra, BobCat, and me

Bobby III, Amaryllis, Cassius, BobCat, Bobby, Kyra, Aidan, Finn, Conor, and me when Bobby announced his presidential run

(left) The yak in Bhutan. (right) The yak running away from Bobby (Bobby's shadow in foreground).

Bobby and me with the Tiger's Nest behind us

"Okay, okay. I'm really glad you told me. I know this must be scary, but you'll never admit it, so I'll stop asking you. Well, I really love you, Paul. It sounds like you're ready for this, so that's good."

"And I really love you too. This time tomorrow, I'll be good as new," Paul said.

We all hugged while Eddie and I choked back our tears. Paul would've been furious if he saw any waterworks.

The brain surgery seemingly went well, Paul persisted in his sunny assessments. Back at home he said he never felt better. Then, strange things started happening. Paul would call me at all hours of the night and talk rather manically. He called at three in the morning to let me know he was outside landscaping his apartment building.

"It's crazy how they let these weeds come in like this," he said.

"Why are you doing that in the middle of the night?" I asked.

"I can't sleep. I don't want to. I have so much energy and I don't want to wake up Eddie, so I thought this would be a good time to do it. And it is! Nobody is around to bother me."

"Um, okay" I said. "It's kinda weird, but . . ."

"It's not weird, Cheryl," he protested. "I'm helping the entire building right now. The neighbors aren't going to believe how much better it looks."

"Paul, I have to go to work in a few hours. Good night, baby."

"Good night, sweet lady," he said.

I was on the ABC show, *Suburgatory*, at that time. I had a lot on my plate between motherhood, a long-distance relationship with Bobby, and shooting the show, but I seemed to have been managing it all. Paul Beckett's post-surgery manic behavior proved to be a new challenge though. He would send me articles about Bobby's family history in the middle of the night. Story after story about John Kennedy, Ted Kennedy, and Bobby's father,

Robert Kennedy. He also fixated on Hollywood celebrities. He'd call me from TV shoots while he was doing extra work and put different actors on the phone. Some I had never met before. It was almost always awkward. I insisted that he stop, but he didn't. I finally had to set hard boundaries with him. He wasn't allowed to call or text after 11:00 p.m. unless it was an emergency, and he wasn't allowed to hand the phone to random people to talk to me anymore. It was discombobulating.

"Paul, what does your doctor say about your state of mind? It seems like you never sleep," I asked.

"Why don't you want me to be happy? This is the happiest I've ever been in my life. Why would I need to talk to a doctor?" he asked.

"I mean, what do they say in your follow up visits? Is this normal?" I asked.

"I don't need to go back. Why do you keep badgering me? Why can't you be happy for me?" Pivoting, he said, "If you want to worry about something, why don't you ask Eddie when he's going to get his heart valve replaced? His doctor said he needs a pig valve. Why don't you focus on that?"

Eddie did have a faulty heart valve, and we often talked about a surgery to replace it, but Eddie was also reticent about doctors. The thought of open-heart surgery terrified him, and Paul's obsession with the idea of replacing Eddie's heart valve with a pig's valve did not comfort him. It was Paul's strategy for diverting the conversation away from his own health issues.

"Let's just talk about you right now. I'm really concerned. You're not yourself," I said.

He brushed it off. "I'm not going to talk about this anymore with you. If you bring it up again, I'll stop talking to you altogether."

One night, in a worried tone, Eddie asked me to come over. When I walked into their apartment, I found Post-it notes covering the walls.

"What's going on?" I asked.

"There are so many things going through my mind," Paul sighed. "I don't want to forget any of it, so I started making notes."

There were notes everywhere reminding him of book titles, health tips, phone numbers, names, and sometimes there would just be single words.

"Wow. Okay. Paul, this is a lot." I said.

"I've got a system. These are all very important. Eddie's not allowed to touch them," he said.

"He doesn't even sleep in our room anymore. He says my breathing keeps him awake," Eddie said.

"It does. I never noticed it before, but now it's all I can think about if I'm lying next to him. It's really loud," Paul complained.

I could see the fear in Eddie's eyes. Eddie was always the quiet, sweet, emotional one of the two. Paul was strong, loud, and funny. Now his humor had abandoned him, eclipsed by the mania.

A month later, Paul took a turn. He crashed from his high and plunged into a deep, dark depression. He became impatient, even mean. He insisted Eddie move out. Eddie was broken-hearted but complied.

"Paul, you've got to go see a doctor. Please. You've been through so much, there's no way you can manage this on your own," I begged.

"If you say that again, I'll hang up on you. I'm just a little down right now," he told me.

"I've known you for most of your life. This is really extreme," I said.

"I've gotta go. Bye, sweet lady," he said as he hung up.

Days later, I got an early morning call from a badly shaken Eddie.

"Cheryl, you've got to come quick. Paul cut his wrists last night. He checked himself into a hotel downtown. They found him in the bathtub. Oh my god. Oh my god."

"What? What are you saying?" I asked, stunned.

I got dressed and drove to the hospital as fast as I could. "My name is Cheryl Hines. My friend said he left my name with you," I said to the emergency room receptionist.

"Okay, Ms. Hines. Please have a seat and we'll be right with you," she said with no urgency in her voice.

I looked around the crowded waiting room. "No, you don't understand. My friend, Eddie, is waiting for me. I need to see him," I said frantically.

"Please have a seat, ma'am," she said.

I stepped back a few feet, but I couldn't sit. My adrenaline was pumping. I kept looking at the clock and then looking back at her. I couldn't hold it in any longer. I went back up to the window and blurted out, "Can you just tell me if Paul Beckett is alive or not!"

There was a hush in the room. Then a security guard came through a door and told me to follow him. My heart was beating loudly. Everything was blurry. My eyes couldn't focus on anything. When he opened the door to another waiting room, I saw Eddie. "What's happening? Tell me what's happening," I asked.

I could tell Eddie had been crying for a long time. Through his tears he said, "He's in surgery. He's been in there for hours. I'm just waiting for the doctor to tell me if he's going to make it."

We waited and waited and waited. Finally, the doctor came out and said, "Your friend is lucky. We were able to save his hands. He had cut his wrists so badly, we had to reattach nerves and arteries. We've been working on him for over six hours," he said.

"Oh my god, thank you," I replied. Eddie couldn't speak.

"He's going to be in traction for a while. He won't be able to use his hands at all until they've had time to heal," he continued.

"Okay. That's okay." I said.

The doctor walked off as Eddie and I sobbed with relief. Eddie told me Paul had taken all of his money out of his bank account and left a money order for him. He had taken everything he owned out of their apartment and had also left Eddie a very short, sweet love note. Eddie was a wreck. His pale, thin frame looked dangerously fragile.

A little while later, they told us we could see Paul. He was sitting up a little bit in his bed, and both of his arms were in casts. They were extended out in front of him and propped up above his heart. There were lots of tears from me and Eddie, but Paul was oddly cheerful.

"Can you believe it? It's like I get a second chance in life," Paul said,

"Paul! What happened?" I asked.

"Well, I was just feeling so down, and I knew it wasn't going to change, I wasn't going to feel any better, so I decided to check myself into a hotel. I didn't want Eddie to find me or anything," he started.

"Oh my god," Eddie whispered.

"And I started cutting my wrists in the bathtub. I was bleeding, but not enough, you know, so I kept cutting and cutting. So much time had gone by and nothing was really happening," he said.

"Oh my god," I whispered.

"So I cut some more and then I finally had to call 911. I don't know what time it was, but I had been in there for a long time and I was afraid I wasn't going to die. I mean, I just wasn't dying. I didn't know what to do. It was such a mess. I'm so sorry," he said.

"It's okay," Eddie said.

"We're just glad you're okay," I said.

"Well, I'm so embarrassed. Look at me. What am I supposed to say to people when they ask me what happened?" he asked.

I thought it was interesting that *that* was his biggest concern.

"Tell them it was a ski accident," I said.

"Yeah, that's good. But how did I break both of my arms?" He asked.

"I guess you fell forward," Eddie said.

"Yeah, I must've come out of my skis. Okay? If anyone asked, we were skiing, I hit a branch or something and I was thrown out of my skis," he confirmed.

Eddie and I looked at each other.

I half-heartedly said, "All right."

Eddie quietly said, "Okay."

So that was settled. Now what about the other important thing? Like living? What about that part?

"Paul . . ." I said.

"Cheryl, don't. I know what you're going to say, and you don't need to. I'm so grateful I didn't die. You guys don't need to worry about this. I learned my lesson. I see everything differently now. I'm happy to be alive. I really did learn from this," he said.

Bobby flew in the next day, and we went to visit Paul.

"Bobby! Oh my god, you didn't have to come," Paul said.

"Of course I wanted to come. I'm happy to see you. Really happy to see you, man." Bobby said sincerely.

"I'm sure Eddie told you I was in a ski accident," Paul said jokingly.

We all gave an awkward chuckle.

"You're the happiest depressed person I've ever seen, Paul," Bobby said.

"I'm just happy to be alive. I see everything completely differently now. I feel very lucky," Paul replied.

Paul's spirits remained high for the duration of his hospital stay. He reassured everyone from the cleaning staff to the doctors that he was back on a good track. He was so convincing they discharged him without ever having any follow-up psychological therapy. When the doctor told Eddie and me we could take Paul home, I followed him down the hall.

"What? We can't take him home. He just tried to kill himself a few days ago. What are we supposed to do about that?" I asked.

"I'm just letting you know that, physically, he's ready to go home," the doctor told me.

"But don't you need to keep him here to make sure he's okay? What's to keep him from doing this again? How can we just take him home?" I pleaded.

"He talked to a psychologist, and both the doctor and Paul feel confident he doesn't require any more help. We can't keep him here against his will," the doctor said firmly and then walked off.

We took Paul home. Eddie, our friends, and I made schedules designating who would stay with Paul. He needed twenty-four-hour care because he couldn't use either of his hands.

Paul kept insisting he was fine and hated the attention he was getting from us. It was hard for me to take overnight shifts, which Paul wouldn't have allowed anyway. He couldn't bear the thought of me seeing him as weak and helpless.

The next few days went relatively well. Paul was in good spirits and reassured us he was grateful for another shot at life. He was doing so well, in fact, he convinced Eddie to take a night off so he could get some rest and persuaded me to go on the spring break ski trip I had planned with Bobby, Paul Young, and the kids. Our friend Jon volunteered to stay with Paul.

Eddie and I called and texted each other nonstop, consumed with worry. I was checking my phone every few minutes, then I allowed myself to take a run on the slopes. When I got to the bottom, I checked my messages and there were several missed calls from Eddie. I called him back immediately. "Cheryl, Cheryl, Cheryl," Eddie said in a low, far away voice.

"Eddie? What happened?" I asked.

"Cheryl, Cheryl, Cheryl," he continued.

"Eddie? What's going on?" I pleaded.

"Cheryl, he did it. Cheryl. Cheryl," Eddie kept repeating.

"Where are you?" I asked.

"I don't know," he said.

"Do you see anyone near you?" I asked.

"Yes," he whispered.

"Can you hand the phone to that person?" I asked.

"Hello?" A man said.

"Hi. You're with my friend, Eddie. Can you tell me where you are?" I asked.

"Yes ma'am. We're in the security office. I'm a security officer," he said somberly.

"I think my friend is in shock. Can you tell me what happened?" I asked.

"Ma'am, there's been an incident involving a male jumping off of the top of the parking garage," he said.

"Oh my god. Oh my god. Is he alive?" I asked.

"Ma'am, I'm not at liberty to say. The LAPD is here now," he said.

"You can't tell me what's going on?" I asked.

"I'm sorry, ma'am," he said.

"Can you tell me this? Was he taken away in an ambulance?" I asked.

There was a long pause. "No ma'am," he said. "It's a matter for the LAPD."

"Oh my god. Is there someone named Jon there?" I asked.

"No ma'am. Just your friend," he replied.

"Okay, thank you. Can someone stay with him until I can arrange for him to be picked up?" I asked.

"Yes, ma'am," he said.

"Thank you. Can you hand the phone back to Eddie, please?" I asked.

"Cheryl?" Eddie said.

"Eddie, I'm going to have someone pick you up and take you to my house. I'll be there as soon as I can. I love you," I told him.

I hung up and realized I was kneeling in the snow in front of my hotel. I'm not sure how I made it back to my hotel room, but Bobby, Paul Young, and a few of the kids were there. Paul immediately booked a flight for me back to LA. Bobby drove me to the airport as I called my new assistant in LA. I thought it was best for the kids to stay with Bobby and Paul.

"Christina, what are you doing right now? I need you to do something very important right this second," I said.

"Anything," she said as she walked out of the beauty salon where she was about to get her hair done.

"I need you to immediately drive to the mall and go to the security office. Something tragic has happened and my friend Eddie is there by himself. He's in shock and can barely speak. Please pick him up and take him to my house. I'll be there as soon as I can." I said.

"I'm on my way right now," she assured me.

"Thank you," I said as I hung up.

Without ever meeting Eddie before, Christina went to pick him up. She found her way to the security office and saw someone who matched the description I had given her. She asked if his name was Eddie and told him I had sent her. He hugged her for a long time without speaking and then got into her car. Christina wasn't even supposed to be working that day, but she showed up and gracefully shouldered a very intense situation. I'm forever grateful for her kindness.

I finally had a chance to talk to Jon. He had taken Paul to get coffee. Paul was to find a table while Jon waited in line. Instead, Paul ran to the top of the parking garage and jumped. Jon searched the outdoor mall and was drawn to a commotion of police lights. Paul had died on impact.

Jon had texted Eddie, but wasn't able to talk to him when he arrived because he was being questioned by the LAPD. Jon was shattered. Besides being overcome with grief, he was angry at Paul. He felt certain Paul had orchestrated this while Eddie and I were away and resented Paul for making him endure such a traumatic experience.

I landed in LA a few hours later and walked into my house to find Eddie, Christina, and some of Eddie's family there. It was the first time I had felt my house filled with sadness. Nobody was sure what to do next. The shock of losing your best friend, in itself is devastating, and the idea of him taking his own life added many more emotional layers none of us were ready to process. We sat in silence for hours. When we were finally able to speak, we started going through the timeline of events. We questioned ourselves about what we could have possibly done differently that might have stopped Paul. We loved him so much and had tried to help in every way we could. We were left with many unanswered questions; the biggest being, *Why couldn't Paul have seen any other way out of his pain?*

We all washed in and out of grief and anger that would alternate in waves for many years. Eventually, I landed on forgiveness and compassion.

Bobby was a pillar of strength for me during that time. Bobby had already inspired me with his ability to find happiness despite the seemingly insurmountable loss he's had in his life. His father was assassinated when he was fourteen years old, and then he lost his two brothers, David and Michael, decades after. Bobby has struggled through the traumatic experiences, but he doesn't carry the bitterness and anger in a way that could easily cast a dark shadow on his life. Having experienced unspeakable losses himself, he knew how to console and be supportive. He spent days and months helping me sort through my grief.

I pushed through the fog of despair to focus on the responsibilities of motherhood and work as best I could. Cat had an extremely close relationship with Paul, and it was hard for her to understand the complexity of the situation at nine years old. It was impossible for me to understand it at forty-eight. Paul and Eddie were with Cat from the day she was born. They taught her how to swim, took her trick-or-treating, and went to her ballet recitals. It was all the worse because Eddie started drifting away. I tried to keep him close, but it was too difficult for him to be with me or in our home because it reminded him of Paul too much.

About eight months later, I received a call from Eddie's sister telling me we had "lost" Eddie due to heart complications. I was completely caught off guard. I had just texted with him, and we had made plans to meet for lunch.

Apparently, Eddie had a cardiac event while he was alone in his apartment. I immediately drove over to his place. I couldn't imagine him not being there, and I guess I needed to see for myself. His door was open and his friend who had found him was sitting on the couch. He told me they had already taken Eddie away. The two of us stayed in his apartment in sad silence surrounded by his artwork, his photos, and his Bohemian clothes as reality sank in. Later, we walked to the bar next door and literally cried in our drinks. He was smoking cigarettes, so I thought I'd join him. We told stories about Eddie as we took long drags from our cigarettes and fanned away the smoke. I went home and threw up all night. Our beautiful Eddie was really gone.

***

Years later, I had what I can only describe as a "visitation" from Paul Beckett. While I was in a twilight state—not quite awake but not yet sleeping—I felt him sitting beside me in my bed. I could see him with a clarity that I had never experienced, although it was more like I was seeing his essence.

He said, "I just wanted to come talk to you while I could still remember how to talk. It's very hard to explain, but, where I am, there's no such thing as talking. It's not the way we communicate."

Paul told me that Eddie had already forgotten how to talk, but he wanted to come and tell me that Eddie's doing great. "He's so happy. And I . . . I just wanted to talk to you before it leaves me, before I can't remember how to do it," he said.

I asked him if he had any regrets. I had in mind his decision to take his own life.

"This is also hard to explain, but, where we are, there's no such feeling as regret. That doesn't exist here. That's something that you guys put on yourselves."

Relieved, I pressed him further. "So, do you wish you would've had kids?"

"No, I had Cat. I really loved being with her and she was everything I ever wanted."

Then, he was gone. Talking to him was very comforting. I had so many questions about how and why everything had happened the way it happened, but in the little time I had with him, I felt myself letting go of them all. Whether it was a dream or something more, I was no longer mad at him for deciding to "leave" us, and it made my heart full to know he and Eddie were happy.

Chapter 13

After losing the two people who had been a central part of my life for the past fifteen years, I was having a hard time adjusting to my new life without them. I needed to go home and be with my family for a while. I knew being with them would be healing. Becky and I were able to visit Paul Beckett's parents in Tallahassee, share stories, and remind them of all the happiness he had brought to our lives.

Bobby met me in Orlando, and we took my niece and nephew, Zoe and Jackson, and Cat to the river for a hike. As we trailed through the trees, the kids were making fun of the way Bobby insisted on listing to them the long inventory of things he loved about me.

"Well, if you love her so much, why don't you marry her?" Jackson said.

And just like that, on the bank of a little Florida lake, Bobby got down on one knee.

"Cheryl, will you marry me?" he asked.

The kids went crazy. They started running around, screaming and cheering.

I looked at Bobby, kind of surprised and said, "Yes, I will marry you."

They were still screaming as Bobby took a string of Spanish moss from a magnolia tree and wrapped it around my neck to make it look more ceremonial. I didn't take the proposal too seriously. It seemed like a spur-of-the-moment gesture egged on by Jackson's dare, so I didn't give it much thought. Months later, when Bobby was back in New York and I was back in LA, we were on the phone, and he asked when I thought we should get married. I was surprised by the question.

"Yeah, I asked you to marry me, remember?" he asked.

"I know, but . . . it was just Spanish moss. I didn't realize it was a *real* proposal," I said.

We had long discussions about the practicalities of this marriage. I loved the idea of becoming a stepmother to his kids. They added a new dimension to my life that I didn't even know I was missing, and Cat adored Bobby. He had taught her how to waterski, catch lizards, and ride a bike. He brought an unpredictable sense of adventure I had never experienced in my life. I loved everything about him, and I knew we were meant to find each other in this lifetime, as odd of a couple as we seemed. We both brought something to the relationship that the other was lacking. I err on the side of caution and prudence. I need to know how deep the water is before I jump off the cliff.

Bobby is the opposite.

***

With Bobby, I never know what's going to happen next. There's always a sense of surprise, of possibility. It reminds me of a quote by Oscar Wilde, which feels especially true when it comes to Bobby: *"The very essence of romance is uncertainty."* That's Bobby. He is extreme in every way. He doesn't do anything halfway—everything he does is *a lot*. If we're hiking in Puerto Rico and there's water nearby, he's not just going to jump in—he's going to do a flip off of the cliff. *What are you doing? You don't even know what's down there!*—I'd find myself saying a lot. But that's just who he is. He doesn't ease into anything. I find it terribly attractive and sometimes maddening, but it's part of what drew me to him.

How can you know how deep the water is until you do a backflip off the cliff and dive down to the bottom?

Though we had agreed to get married, we decided to stay where we were for the time being. I would live in Bel Air with Cat and Kyra—with Kick and Bobby III living close by—and Bobby in New York with Aidan, Finn, and Conor. We would spend the next six months making plans as we sold our houses and bought a place together by the beach.

In the span of a year, I had received a star on Hollywood Boulevard, gotten engaged to Bobby, and lost both of my best friends. How was I going to have a wedding without Paul and Eddie?

Bobby and I thought that we would just go to the courthouse with our kids in Hyannis Port and forego a big wedding. We wanted to have a quiet, intimate ceremony with a small party afterward. I told Ethel about our plan to elope. She couldn't believe we didn't want to have a wedding.

"Well, it's my second marriage, and it's Bobby's third," I told her.

"Yes, but it's your first marriage to each other," she said.

I had to admit, she had a point. She said we should get married on her lawn, in front of the ocean so everyone could be a part of it. The more she talked, the better it sounded. It was impossible to argue with Ethel. I told Bobby what Ethel and I were up to. He liked the idea of having our families together, so we made the decision to have a small wedding at Ethel's.

As the summer went by, I spent a lot of time going over plans with Ethel. She wanted to know what kind of china and crystal we were going to have on the tables. It didn't go over well when I told her it was going to be a casual clambake with paper plates. She was aghast at the paper plate idea, and I never uttered those words again. She also thought the idea of someone having to get up and go to a bar to get their own drink was demoralizing.

She explained that every person should have a crystal water glass, a white wine glass, a red wine glass and a champagne flute at their setting. Ethel and I were having a tough time hammering out the details. She wasn't budging.

Ultimately, I had one table at the reception set with the finest china, silver, and crystal complete with a server standing by. Ethel had the only assigned seat there. Everyone else waited in line for their lobster and beer.

Between Bobby's family and mine, we were already looking at around two hundred people. We didn't tell most people it was a wedding; we just said we were having a clambake, and they should come if they could. Of course, our families knew, but we didn't want word getting out to the media. We didn't make an announcement about our engagement. We were happy with our quiet nuptials.

As the wedding approached, the weather forecast was predicting rain. That meant we would have to move everything inside. The only tent that was able to hold that many people wouldn't fit in front of Ethel's house, so Bobby's cousin Teddy Kennedy Jr. and his wife Kiki graciously offered to host it on their lawn. Squeezed between Bobby and Ethel's yards, Teddy's house served as the summer White House during the Kennedy administration.

It was a beautiful, memorable day. Ethel, my mom and stepfather, Phil, my dad and my stepmother, Helen, all of our siblings and in-laws, our nieces and nephews, and of course, our seven kids stood beside us as we said our *I Do's*.

Ethel was right. It was important for us to share the day with the people we loved the most.

Nothing about the day went quite as planned. I heard my cue to walk down the aisle as they started playing the Bridal Chorus, but Ethel's dog, Heffe, beat me to the punch and ran out before me. *I guess I'll just follow the dog,* I thought as I covered my mouth to hide my laughter and stepped into the tent to see Bobby waiting for me at the end of the aisle.

The night was pure joy, and no one had a better time than little Michael. When the band started playing at the reception, it was a matter of minutes until all of the Hines, Kennedy, and Shriver nieces and nephews had him out of his wheelchair, twirling him around the dance floor. Michael wanted us to get married every year after that.

Bobby's son Conor, then eighteen, gave the most beautiful toast. He had everyone in laughter and then in tears.

***

Once Bobby's six kids were added to the mix, I went from being a mom of an only child to a mom and stepmom of seven. Cat is the youngest of the kids and it was a big adjustment for her to suddenly be a part of such a big family. Even though my stepdaughter, Kyra, is nine years older than Cat, they bonded early.

Cat was only ten when Kyra asked if they could plan a birthday party for me. It was a cute idea. I'm not really the kind of person who wants a birthday party, but I thought it would be a fun project for them. I went into my bedroom to relax and left the girls alone in the living room. Just as I closed my eyes, my phone started pinging. Texts were coming in nonstop. I assumed some sort of international news was breaking. I checked my phone and saw my friend Suzanne had texted: "Wow, that's going to be a lot of animals. Should people bring carrying cages?"

I called her and said, "What are you talking about?"

"I just got an Evite from you. Your birthday pool party? The only gift you want is a pet? It says the more exotic, the better," she said.

I ran into the living room, and Kyra and Cat were beaming.

"What did you do?" I asked.

"We sent out an Evite for your party," Kyra said.

"We're getting a lot of RSVPs already," Cat said.

I looked at the invitation. They had invited all three-hundred-odd people in my contacts. Moms from Cat's preschool I hadn't seen in years, my ex-husband's family in Utah and Colorado, friends in Florida, celebrities I'd worked with, **EVERYONE.** The RSVPs kept flooding in. People were excited about the exotic pet pool party. When I looked closer, I noticed that they'd put the wrong date on the invitation. I seized the opportunity to send out an alert to my party goers.

"I'm so sorry, but there's been a mix up with the date. Cat and Kyra were kind enough to plan a party for me, but there are a few details they didn't quite get right. As much as I'd love to see you all in your bikinis and Speedos holding an exotic pet, I'm going to have to cancel this one."

I knew I was going to need to keep an eye on those two.

***

I didn't expect animals to feature so prominently in our lives. Somehow, they always show up, even on vacation. Early in our marriage, Bobby and I went on a trip to Bhutan that he had arranged for a Waterkeeper fundraiser. I didn't have any expectations. I knew nothing about Bhutan. I was just along for the ride. It turned out that Bhutan is a magical little kingdom on the southern slopes of the eastern Himalayas nestled between India and China. By then, Bobby knew that I wasn't big on hiking or camping. I like a hot shower.

"Remind me to tell you something on the plane," he said.

"Just tell me now, " I said.

"No, no. I'll tell you when we're on the plane," he told me.

I forgot to ask what he wanted to tell me on the flight.

When we landed, we were greeted by our guide, Tshering Tobgay, who later became Bhutan's prime minister. I asked why visitors to Bhutan required a guide. He explained, "This is a very special place, but we've learned it can be dangerous for people who don't know the terrain. We don't want a visitor getting lost in the mountains or falling off a cliff. In the case of an emergency, you would need someone who knows the land." What Bobby had intended to tell me on the plane was that we would be trekking across the Himalayas and camping in tents. "It can be difficult to get medical attention in Bhutan," Tobgay added. "There is only one helicopter here."

"In the whole country?" I asked.

"Yes, but it's a small country," he replied.

Bhutan is a devoutly Buddhist country that has steadfastly resisted Western values and money. It discourages tourism and polluting industries. Bhutan doesn't gauge its success, as every other nation does, by Gross National Product (GNP), but by Gross National Happiness (GNH). Maybe we all have something to learn from Bhutan.

Bobby had not expected that we were going on the Himalayan trek. He had only said that we were going to see the Tiger's Nest Monastery, also known as the Paro Takstang, the most iconic and sacred temple in Bhutan. Built in 1692, it was inspired by Guru Rinpoche, the spiritual master who brought Buddhism to Bhutan in the eighth century. According to legend, he flew to this remote cliffside on the back of a flying tigress and then meditated in a cave for three years, three months, three weeks, three days, and three hours. I was intrigued by the idea of a magical tigress and was excited to see this historical monastery. I didn't realize it was on the side of a cliff, three thousand feet above the Paro Valley.

I was only told to pack an overnight bag. We arrived at the bottom of a mountain where a few men with donkeys awaited. We gave them our bags, and they headed up a steep hill. I looked around, noting that I was the only one who brought a purse. I barely had time to process that thought before we immediately started hiking up a very steep incline. I quickly realized that I didn't need my purse.

The climb to the mountain was steep and arduous. From atop the hills, the tiny houses in the green valleys below looked as if their roofs were painted red, as locals had meticulously laid harvested red chili peppers out to dry. The effect was charming, beautiful, and practical. I was surprised to see that many of the houses had murals of giant penises, which is a popular religious symbol in Bhutan. Sometimes I found that it distracted from the countryside's natural beauty, while others in our group celebrated every mural.

About eight hours into the climb, our friend, the alpine ski legend, Klaus Heidegger, pointed to the top of the mountain and said happily in his Austrian accent, "That's where we're going!"

Klaus's daughter, Nicoletta, and I looked at each other and laughed. We were exhausted and glad we had stopped to catch our breath. We were looking around for our campsite, hoping it was not more than a few more feet.

"But, seriously," I asked, "How much further?"

"I am serious, that's where we'll sleep tonight, and tomorrow we'll hike over to Tiger's Nest," he said. "The guide said that it was only about six more hours if we hurry, in which case we could make it before dark."

"Are you friggin' kidding me?" Nicoletta asked.

Bobby added, "Oh yeah, that's what I was going to tell you on the plane."

"What?" I asked.

"It's a fifteen-hour hike, but we're getting to do what very few people ever have the chance to do. Climb to the top. There's a Bhutan Sky Burial cemetery where vultures devour the dead up there," Bobby said happily. "We get to camp right next to it!"

Nicoletta and I looked at each other with disbelief, terror, and rage.

"Bobby! Oh my god! We can't go that far! We've barely made it here," I said.

"Yes you can. I know you can, but I didn't want you to talk yourself out of trying," he said.

"Bobby!" I yelled.

Unscripted

"Let me track down one of the donkeys, and I'll get you some more water and maybe a little something to eat," he tried to calm me.

The next four hours were excruciating. Bobby walked behind me and literally had to push my ass up that unbelievably steep mountain. Occasionally, during the ordeal, he tried to console me with Betel nut, a mild stimulant chewed by the locals which makes their teeth and lips black. I declined. We made it to the top, and there sat a beautiful campsite with white tents, strings of colorful prayer flags, and the donkeys that had hauled our food and clothes. I was relieved and was ready to relax. I really was hoping to call it a day.

Just as everyone was unpacking and getting settled, Bobby grabbed me by the hand, "Let's go look around before it gets dark."

I hadn't even had time to sit down but thought maybe I could push through a little more to see a beautiful sunset, so we peeled off to explore. We were only about a half mile from the campsite when we noticed a two-thousand-pound wild yak with giant horns walking steadily towards us with an angry stare. Bobby started laughing. Eyes locked in, the yak lumbered towards us menacingly.

"Are yaks dangerous?" I whispered.

"I'm not sure," he said. The yak began its charge in earnest.

"Maybe you should get inside that cage," Bobby said, pointing to a dilapidated wooden corral. Before I was able to get inside, the yak charged Bobby.

"Yeah, it's dangerous," he said matter-of-factly.

I couldn't believe what I was seeing. He was being attacked by a yak in Bhutan. My thoughts went to the one helicopter in the country! I closed my eyes. I couldn't watch. Bobby was recording all of this with his phone. When the yak got close to him, Bobby slapped the animal's nose with his phone. When I opened my eyes, the yak was running away. It stopped and turned back to cast an evil stare at Bobby.

Nearby was a ruin of a centuries-old broken stone wall about waist high.

"Come on, honey, get on the other side of that stone wall. Get on the other side of the stone wall quickly," he said.

The yak looked like it was going to charge again. Its eyes were locked on Bobby.

"Come on. Get behind it," he said.

Trying not to anger the yak even more, I gingerly crept over to the wall with my walking stick and my crossbody purse.

"This is crazy," I whispered.

Bobby laughed again.

"It's not funny," I whispered.

"Let's make a run for it," he said.

"No, I think he'll chase us if we run," I whispered.

We waited it out. We stood quietly until the yak felt sure we weren't a threat and wandered off. I don't recall getting to see the sunset.

That night we had dinner with the group, told stories by the fire, and slept in a tent on top of the world. I'd never seen so many stars or experienced such quiet and calm. We were bewitched by the beauty of Bhutan and the Tiger's Nest.

We only had to survive a yak attack to get there.

We spent the next few days hiking along a high-altitude ridgeline trail from one Buddhist temple, or Lhakhang, to another, finally arriving at the Tiger's Nest on the last day.

***

While I appreciated Bobby's survival skills, I always had a slight fear that one day we'd be in the middle of nowhere, my appendix would burst, and Bobby would happily perform an emergency appendectomy with a pocketknife. (I still wouldn't rule it out.) I had an eye-opening validation of this worry that only reinforced my fear while skiing with the kids. I was with Cat, Zoe, Jackson, Griffin, and my niece Tori. They were all pretty young, between nine and thirteen. We were on the ski slope in a whiteout blizzard. The kids were cold and scared. To bolster their courage, I promised them hot chocolate once we got to the bottom of the slope. We carefully skied down to a little hotel, and ordered hot chocolate before realizing I didn't have any money. I knew it was time to be resourceful, so I approached a table of strangers.

"Hi. Could any of you possibly lend me some money? I'm good for it, I'll pay you back. I'm just trying to get hot chocolate to calm the kids down."

"Are you with Bobby Kennedy?" one of them asked.

"I am," I said.

"You know, I was camping with him in a Peruvian jungle one time and cut my leg. It was a big cut, and Bobby sewed it up with dental floss," he said, handing me a wad of money. "No need to pay me back, because I still owe him. Tell him I said hi."

"Well, that sounds about right," I said. "Thank you so much."

It made me consider a preemptive appendectomy in the states.

***

Is today the day I wake up and kill an emu with a shovel? How did I get here? Why do I have an emu living in my backyard? And why does the emu hate me so much? These are the questions I asked myself every day for the two years of our marriage that I lived in Malibu. I never imagined myself living in Malibu or having an emu.

Cat loved animals when she was younger. When Bobby and I got married, she had mixed feelings about adopting a large, blended family. In an effort to win her over, Bobby gave her a baby emu. She named him Tobias, but we all called him Toby for short. He started out around six inches tall and absolutely adorable. A few months later, Toby was a strapping six feet. He slept outside of Cat's room at night and made a strange, booming drumming sound she found relaxing. The older he got, the less he liked anyone other than Cat and Bobby.

Somehow, Cat taught him to sit. Let's just say, he had no such respect for me. He *definitely* didn't even like me and if I'm being perfectly honest, I wasn't crazy about him.

Toby would chase people across the yard on giant legs, galloping in pursuit of human prey like a velociraptor with his tiny head bobbing on his long neck. Whenever someone ventured across the lawn towards the pool, you could watch the chase from the comfort of the couch. It was hilarious. But if you were the one being chased, it was a real pressure cooker. We had an acre of land for him to run around but when there was no one to chase, he preferred to wait for human company. He would stand outside of the sliding glass living room door, waiting for an opportunity to enter. Sometimes, the dogs would open the door for Toby.

One day, Bobby came home from work and looked over my shoulder at my computer screen: the subject line was "lifespan of emus." It was ten to twenty years, and thirty-five in captivity. I was heartsick. I didn't tell Bobby how often I'd searched the term.

It got to the point where I couldn't go into the backyard without carrying a shovel for protection. I'd take Ronan, our big Gordon Setter, with me, but after a while, even that didn't help.

Toby would only chase me faster because Ronan was chasing him. All I wanted was to wake up in the morning and drink my coffee in the backyard by the roses. I'd often find myself, coffee in one hand and a shovel in the other thinking, *Is today the day I kill Toby? Is that how my day is going to start?*

I started getting resentful. I had written a screenplay and was waiting for a call from a producer so we could talk about financing the film. The call came in but I wasn't getting good reception in the house, so I stepped outside. I started pitching the film, "It's about a woman who gets divorced and starts dating again . . ." and then Toby came at me, full charge.

I didn't have my shovel *or* Ronan. As the giant bird chased me around, I tried to keep my voice calm as I continued my conversation. I thought for a moment, *Do I tell this producer I'm being chased by an emu?* I decided against it. I didn't want to sound crazy and unfocused. Why would someone pitch a film while they're being chased by an emu?

I tried to sound measured as I ran. "Anyway, it's a comedy about jumping into the dating world again . . ."

I finally managed to wrangle Toby into the house and shut the sliding glass door. Out of breath, I finished with, "and, ultimately finding love again in an unexpected place."

The producer didn't seem impressed. We ended the call, and I stood outside, glaring at Toby standing in my living room. When Bobby got home, I let him have it. "It's Toby or me. One of us is going."

"Just say the word," Bobby said.

"I've said the word. Several times," I yelled.

"Sorry, honey. I always thought you were kidding," he said.

"Yeah, I know. It *sounds* funny because I'm complaining about being chased by an emu—but it's not funny," I said.

So, Bobby found a kind woman in Malibu with a big ranch who was happy to take Toby. She told me I could visit him whenever I wanted. "That won't be necessary, but thank you."

Chapter 14

On March 15, 2018, I received another life-changing phone call, this time from Chris's wife April. There was no easy way to say it—she told me that my brother had suddenly died of a heart attack. I refused to believe her. Still in shock herself, she recounted what had happened.

They were at the gym in cycling class, when he stepped out saying he wasn't feeling well. As she drove him to the hospital, he went into cardiac arrest. She pulled over to vainly give him CPR. The doctors later told her he had had what is called a "widow-maker." The more details she gave, the more I realized everything she was telling me had to be true.

I wished I hadn't answered the phone. I wished I didn't know. I wanted my life back from two minutes before when I thought Chris was still alive. Somehow, I managed to call my mother, Becky, and Mike to tell them the devastating news. Time stopped and nothing mattered anymore.

I looked up to see Cat staring at me with grave concern. It snapped me back. I remembered that there were other things that *did* still matter.

"Mom, are you okay?" she asked.

I wasn't okay. I could barely breathe. I couldn't move. I didn't want to scare her by telling her the truth. The truth was, I was not okay, and I didn't think I would ever be okay again. She was just a kid though and I'm her mom. I'm supposed to take care of her, to be strong for her, but I was so overwhelmed, I could only think about Chris. There wasn't room in my thoughts for anything else.

I couldn't lie to her.

"I'm not okay at the moment. I just need a second."

I was going to need more than a second. I was struggling with the reality of Chris being gone. I couldn't accept it. I started unraveling. I couldn't focus my thoughts. The heaviness was setting in.

***

I talked to Chris every day. During my long drives around LA, I'd call him, and he and little Michael would entertain me. Chris was one of the few people I ever talked to about politics. He was a Republican and I was a Democrat. We had such different world views, but we still loved our conversations. I was always curious to know why he felt the way he did and vice versa. We'd spend hours trying to convince each other to cross over to the other side. It never turned heated or hateful. We knew it wasn't black and white. We had shared values in all of the gray spaces between our extremes. I couldn't imagine my world without him.

Bobby and I immediately flew to Florida to be with my family. Few people are more compassionate during a time of grief than Bobby. It's almost as if he transforms into a different version of himself. Usually, he has a big presence, but he becomes smaller, almost invisible. He has a way of being helpful, doing little things that most people aren't able to think about in those dark moments. I've watched him do dishes, take out the trash, or just quietly embrace the person in the room who hadn't had the strength to pick up their head and speak to anyone.

As our family gathered to plan the unthinkable, a memorial to say good-bye to our brother, Bobby was especially helpful with Michael. Michael absolutely adored Bobby and was happily distracted as Bobby took him out on the boat, gave him a bath, got him ready for bed, and told him story after story while the rest of us gathered in the kitchen and tried to come up with a plan of how to support Griffin and Michael through the crushing transition of losing their father.

Michael had always been Chris's Little Buddy. Chris had become skilled at powerlifting Michael in and out of his wheelchair. He knew all of Michael's little quirks and was constantly rearranging leg braces and devices, playing his favorite music, calling Aunt Becky at all hours of the day or night per Michael's whim. It was a 24/7 responsibility and Chris insisted on being at Michael's side for every minute of it. It was extremely challenging, both physically and emotionally, but Michael's love for Chris was all Chris needed to keep him inspired and propel him, gladly, through the next onerous task.

The next day, Michael began to understand that Chris was gone. Unable to verbally express his grief, he started having extreme seizures and was hospitalized. It was almost as if he had decided he didn't want to live without his dad. His body was giving out. The medical staff worked around the clock to stabilize him. When he was able to speak again, he kept calling out for his dad. We took turns staying with Michael in his hospital room and stepping outside to plan Chris's memorial. It all felt like more than we could bear.

When Bobby, Cat, and I finally returned home to LA, I was struck down by grief. I couldn't get out of bed. Darkness enveloped the universe, and I couldn't see any way out. Seeking a road through the pain, I read and reread, *On Death and Dying*, by Elisabeth Kübler-Ross. The book was helpful, but what I really wanted to know was how much longer it was going to be until I would be able to get out of bed. Was there ever going to be a time when I wouldn't be paralyzed by grief? I felt like if I had a timeline, maybe I would be able to endure my depression.

Bobby was taking good care of me, but I really needed answers. He had lost two brothers and his cousin John, who had been like a brother to him. I thought, if anyone would know, it would be him.

"How much longer do I feel like this before it gets better?" I asked.

He just looked at me and hugged me. I thought, *Oh no, this can't be good.* He had no answer for me. He didn't try to talk me into feeling better, he just made me feel loved.

The truth is—there is no answer. There's no timeline. Grief stays with you. One day you wake up and you're able to have a thought that's not about your loss. And then, one day you wake up and have two thoughts that's not about your loss. It's a slow and painful process with setbacks that lead you back to square one. But you realize that you have to go on. Eventually, you find your footing. I never thought it would happen, but in the course of time, I found a way to carry the loss of Chris with me as I resumed my life again.

Chapter 15

My life had gotten back on track, and my family was thriving as well—until March 2020 when the pandemic brought everything to an abrupt halt. The media and every respected authority warned us that the deadly contagious disease, COVID-19, was spreading quickly and everyone would need to stay in place and lock down.

Conor, Finn, Kyra, and Aidan moved in with Cat, Bobby, and me. With seven of us living together, we learned to adjust to our new, intimate living situation. We were used to being together for weeks at a time during holidays, so we felt confident we could ride it out as the kids finished their school semesters online and some of us worked from home. What we thought would be a few weeks, turned into months. It was uncertain how long we would need to stay locked down as news of the disease grew more dire. I found it nearly impossible to keep anxiety at bay as I watched the death tickers on the news outlets tally the fatalities.

During that stressful period, my friends and I tried to distract ourselves by playing online games of Mafia and poker with each other. Cat and Kyra scrolled through social media, the boys watched every movie ever made, and Bobby worked furiously night and day demanding information from government officials as to how they were making decisions about the lockdowns and school closures.

With so many of us in the house together, it was hard to have a moment of privacy. I was going crazy listening to everyone talking on speaker phone while podcasts blared throughout the house simultaneously. The only way I was able to have a private call was by sitting in my car. I was in the driveway, on the phone with my therapist when Kyra knocked on the window.

"Cher, what're you doing out here?" she asked.

"I'm talking to my therapist," I said.

"OK, can I sit with you?" she asked.

"I'd really just like to have a moment alone with him, if you don't mind," I said.

"Why can't I sit with you? Are you talking about me or something?" she asked.

"No, but I'd like to have the option to," I said.

"Cher!" she said.

"I'm just kidding. I'm trying to figure out the meaning of life, and I just need a few minutes," I said.

"Okay. Call me when you're done. I'll come back out and sit with you for a while, and you can tell me everything he says."

"Okay, I will."

"Love you," she said.

"Love you too," I said.

As soon as I rolled up the window, she tapped on it again.

"Yes?" I asked.

"What do you think we should do about dinner?"

"Kyra! He's on the clock," I said.

"Okay, okay. Call me," she said as I rolled the window back up.

***

The pandemic seemed to bring out the best and the worst in people. On one hand, we saw communities coming together, encouraging each other to stay strong and take care of their loved ones. Medical workers were risking their lives every day by going to work to help those in need. And on the other hand, we saw people fighting in public places because they didn't like the way someone was wearing their mask or not wearing one at all. There were definitely aspects of it that didn't seem to make sense. You had to wear a mask on the plane, but you could pull it down, take a bite of food and pull it back up. I would've done anything at that point to avoid creating more anxiety for someone else though, so I just went along with the rules.

Bobby and I began veering off into separate directions. He was focused on the repercussions of the fast-moving decisions that were being made and what effect they would have on society and public health. I was focusing more on the micro effect of the lockdown. I was concerned about Cat missing her last years in high school, how our kids were coping with the stress of the situation, and how I would manage shooting our last season of *Curb* during the pandemic. My fear of possibly getting someone else sick was overwhelming.

Soon the idea of a vaccine that would prevent transmission of the disease was introduced. It ignited acrimonious debates between doctors, scientists, activists, families, and friends. Some people were counting down the days until they could receive the vaccine, while others wanted more information before they had to get it. Bobby emerged as a leader among the people who wanted proof that it was safe and effective. I'm sure most of us can recall the fever pitch of the vaccine debate. People on both sides were loud and highly emotional.

Amidst all the grim talk of death and disease, I managed to find a new diversion that could make me laugh until I cried. Comedian Tig Notaro and I launched the *Tig & Cheryl: True Story* podcast. We would watch a documentary and then spend an hour loosely describing it. Our conversation tended to wander off on frivolous detours, and frankly, we seldom provided our audience with important details of the film or any profound insights.

We never pretended to be anything other than a nonsensical interlude for people who needed a break from lockdown madness. Our listeners found in it a whimsical detour from the pain, loneliness, and despair. Sometimes Tig didn't even watch some of the documentaries. About as deep as we got was in concluding, during our *The Inventor* podcast, (the Elizabeth Holmes story), that Ms. Holmes had created a $9 billion herpes detector. We would end each episode with a question that everyone should ask themselves after watching a serious documentary about Ponzi schemes, cults, or murder—*Who were you attracted to?*

The questions and reviews from our listeners—while we read and dissected for all—were comedy gold. They called themselves Snerkbols. Somehow, over the *LuLaRich* episode, I misread the name on one of our fan mail submissions as "Snerkbol" instead of "Sneaker Boi." If you asked any of our listeners—*Are you a Snerkbol?* They would answer—*You bet your sweet ass I am.* We had created our own language. We formed a special bond with our audience. The world may have been ending, but I was going down with the Snerkbols and that made everything okay.

***

Unscripted

I moved out of my house to self-quarantine while I was shooting *Curb*. I became a recluse in my little apartment in Santa Monica. I got the vaccine as I was required to do for work. Shortly after, I got Covid anyway. I was glad I wasn't with Bobby at the time. I knew that if I'd been living at home with him, somehow he would've been blamed for giving me Covid.

I would've been content to never have another discussion about vaccines again, but that wasn't going to be the case. It seemed to be the only thing people wanted to talk about. Some were furious at Bobby for questioning the safety and efficacy of the vaccine. "He's putting us all at risk." Then there were others coming up to me in tears, telling me to thank Bobby for the important work he was doing.

It reminded me of paintball in Moscow, being trapped behind the log, unable to speak the language, dreading getting shot between the eyes with a paintball pellet from an ex-KGB member.

***

Even though the pandemic resulted in a lot of businesses and schools shutting down, I was able to work. We shot *The Flight Attendant*, following extremely strict Covid protocols. While I was grateful to be on the critically acclaimed show and loved working with the incredible cast and crew, my homelife was becoming more stressful.

Bobby was invited on podcasts and news outlets that shared his concerns about the handling of the pandemic. Half the world loved him. The other half despised him. Joe Rogan introduced him on his podcast saying, "Buckle your seatbelts, everyone. This episode is going to make a lot of people mad." The mainstream media demonized him and often misstated his views and mischaracterized his statements. I found myself frustrated with Bobby every time a news story broke reporting something divisive he supposedly said. Many times, a quote would be taken out of context to ignite a fiery story. I started to care less if it was taken out of context or not, sometimes I didn't like the language he used. I was aggravated that he'd say anything that had the chance of being taken out of context.

The hostility toward him within my industry became deafening. People warned me about losing work. Some of my friends started to grow distant. A few of them disapproved of Bobby so intensely that it became too emotionally challenging for them to stay close.

As Bobby continued to rattle cages, I began getting heat for choosing to stay married to him. It was around that time that we decided to take a break from recording *Tig & Cheryl: True Story*. Our show was never political. It was only meant to be entertaining, and we did not want to get caught up in the controversial conversations swirling around. I had never felt the sort of genuine, personal connection to so many people before as I had with our listeners, but after 10 million downloads, we said goodbye to the Snerkbols. It was heartbreaking, but it seemed like the right thing to do. Neither Tig nor I wanted to get bogged down in politics. It would prove inevitable for me, though.

Adding to my grief and sense of loss, *Curb Your Enthusiasm* shot its finale. *Curb* had been a big part of my life during my thirties, forties and fifties. Even though I didn't see Larry, Jeff, Susie, Richard, and JB every day, I loved being with them through the years. They felt like family to me and the ending of *Curb* was yet another chapter that was closing.

Bobby could see the toll his outspoken, controversial stances were beginning to have on me. He pitched me on the idea of a fake separation. If the world thought we were separated, people would be less inclined to blame and attack me for his actions. In a *New York Times* article, he later explained, "I saw how it was affecting her life, and I said to her, 'We should just announce that we are separated,' so that you can have some distance from me." I didn't think a fake separation would solve any of our problems. I imagined paparazzi lurking around, trying to get photos of us together so they could break a story about how we actually *weren't* separated. I also took our kids into consideration.

Although they were all young adults, certainly capable of understanding complicated situations, I didn't want to add more stress on them. My bonds with each of them kept getting stronger as we shared the bunker together. I deeply appreciated the late-night talks with Finn, Aidan, and Conor around the kitchen island. Their wisdom and humor fortified me. They saw the world with an admirable detachment that allowed them to interpret what was happening from a bird's-eye point of view. They would advise me not to take things personally. I was hoping I could weather the storm with Bobby and the kids by my side. I thought we could all move through it together and take care of each other. Any animosity that was coming toward me was a drop in the bucket compared to what was coming at Bobby daily, but he always seemed ready for the fight. It was wearing on me.

My siblings started to worry about me. We had seen our share of hard times together, but they had never seen me so down for so long. My friends could see a change in me, too. Those I had known longest, my friends from Tallahassee, began reaching out to me with their support. Whether they were Republicans, Independents, or Democrats, it didn't matter. They wanted me to know they still loved me and were thinking about me. A group of us were on a text thread to support each other. Many of them were supportive of Bobby while some disagreed with his views, but they made it clear that their political beliefs were irrelevant to their friendship with him or me.

My life was changing. Chapters were closing. Cat was getting ready to move out and go off to college, and I felt like I was losing my best friend. I became bereft even thinking about life without her.

My friend Debbie, the mother of one of Cat's best friends, Camille, and I started sinking into the sadness about our girls leaving. Cat and Camille tried to ease my anxiety.

"Mom, it's not like we're going off to war or anything," Cat said.

"Yeah, you and my mom are starting to worry us," Camille added.

"We're starting to wonder if we should be depressed about this too. It's hard for us to see you so sad. Are you going to be okay?" Cat asked.

It made me think of my mom and the time when she told me I should move to California and reassured me she was going to be okay without me. Looking back, I realize she probably didn't know if she was going to be okay or not, but she knew it was the best thing for me to do at the time. It was her ultimate gift.

"Of course I'm going to be okay. I'm just trying to get used to the idea of waking up every day and not making you breakfast before school. Seeing your face," I said, as I wiped the tears away.

"Yeah, this is what we're talking about. You're crying about breakfast right now," Cat said.

"Please don't cry about breakfast," Camille said.

"You're right, you're right. This isn't supposed to be a sad time. I'm happy that you girls are going off to school. I really am. You're going to have so much fun," I said as I brought them in for a group hug.

I could feel them trying to end the hug. It was going on for too long.

"Mom, is this what it's going to be like every time we walk into the kitchen?" Cat asked.

"Maybe," I said. "I'll work on it."

Chapter 16

Nothing really prepares a person for the day their spouse asks them, "What do you think about the idea of me running for president?"

"President? Of what?" I asked.

"Of the United States," he said.

"What? Why? . . . What?" I was trying to catch up to what he was saying.

"There's a polling company that has been putting my name in their polls for presidential candidates," he said. "I'm polling pretty high."

This was in May 2022, and it was the first time we had ever talked about polls and polling. I had no idea what kind of role polls would play in our lives for the next twenty-two months. I had so many questions.

"Why would they put you in their polls? How would this even work? Why now?" I asked.

"Well, would you even be open to the idea before we get into all of that? I just wanted to talk to you about it now before I even consider it."

We locked eyes for a long time, trying to find answers in each other's souls. I didn't see this coming. I bristled and felt a flush come over me. It felt like there was a giant wave in front of us that would hit us all at once, take us down to the bottom of the ocean, hold us under until we couldn't breathe, and then spit us out . . . somewhere. Who knew where? Someplace completely unknown. Someplace I've never been before, and I wasn't sure I'd ever want to visit.

"Do I need to give you an answer right now?" I asked.

"Of course not," he said. "I think this will be a long conversation. I need to know how you feel about it. A lot of things would have to fall into place for me to even consider it."

Somehow that last sentiment brought me peace of mind. I thought, *Oh, good. Whew. That was close. Maybe we didn't need to talk about it in a real way. Maybe this was just a "what if" exercise.* As we talked, it was clear the possibility of him running had to be just between the two of us. That was imperative. "Okay, so let's talk about it," I said.

He laid out the reasons he felt compelled to run. It wasn't a desire necessarily, it was more like a calling for him, so, I listened with an open heart and slight terror.

"Well, first of all, I would need to know you're on board. I couldn't do this without you," he said.

"Okay," I said. "Not, *okay* like *'I'm okay with it,'*" I explained. "I'm just saying the word *okay.*"

"Yeah, I got that," he said.

Here's the man I love. I would never want to stand in the way of him reaching his potential, so I kept listening. I couldn't take my eyes off him. I was searching for any indication of just how serious he was about this. I was pretty sure he was dead serious.

During those early months, as he put together his exploratory team, we referred to his potential candidacy as "*The Cookie Company.*" Word couldn't get out that he was considering a presidential run. There were too many components to consider before the press could get wind of his intention. Until the moment he finally went public, we'd have long discussions about opening a cookie company.

***

I was also starting to feel the loss of the relationships I had with Bobby's siblings. Many of them didn't agree with Bobby's views about questioning the safety testing for vaccines. They were concerned about him sowing doubt about the integrity of America's health-care system, with which his family had been deeply involved for generations. I didn't know if the new landscape of their family dynamics would be permanent, but I often thought about the good times we had together. I considered some of them close friends and I wasn't ready for the "new normal" of having distant relationships with my in-laws. The saving grace through it all was my immediate family, though. Becky, Mike, my in-laws, our mom, and all of my nieces and nephews were there for Bobby and me, no matter their political views or the latest headline. They never wavered.

I had constructed my life around entertainment. I never had any desire to be part of a political conversation—or to be married to a polarizing public figure, for that matter—although I suppose no one really aspires to that. I never posted anything political besides encouraging people to vote. I didn't tell them who they should vote for, just that it was important to participate.

As I started to feel consumed by the contentious vaccine discussions Bobby was having daily with disagreeable journalists, I tried to connect with him about it. I wanted to talk to him about the complications his outspoken beliefs were creating for me and the family, but it seemed like our discussions would lead back to him showing me studies and facts and figures about why he had taken up the fight.

As tired as I was of hearing about it, I could understand the two sides of the vaccine argument. I've always struggled with the idea that doctors and scientists could develop something intended to improve the health of millions, yet a pharmaceutical company might uncover issues with that product and choose not to act. It felt inconceivable to me. I worried that Bobby's political campaign would get bogged down in the vaccine debate. It struck me how both sides of the vaccine safety debate—those who say vaccines are proven safe and shouldn't be questioned, and those who believe we should continue studying them to ensure safety—are ultimately motivated by the same goal: protecting children's health.

I recall having an unsolicited conversation about this with one of Bobby's family members in the *don't question them* camp who pointed out that there will always be collateral damage with any drug given to millions of people. I asked her if she would have the same attitude about it if it were her child that was the collateral damage. And what if the collateral damage is in great numbers? Isn't it worth looking for a way to reduce the numbers?

When I met Bobby, he was an environmental attorney and his work shaped much of his life. He spent decades digging into how toxic exposures from chemicals in our water, and pesticides in our soil can quietly erode human health. A few years back, I watched him and his legal team take on one of the biggest players in agribusiness: Monsanto.

They weren't representing a class-action lawsuit or a sweeping coalition—just one man, Dewayne Johnson, a school groundskeeper who'd spent years spraying Roundup as part of his job. Eventually, he developed Non-Hodgkin's Lymphoma. What came out during the trial was chilling—internal emails showed that Monsanto had known about the potential health risks linked to glyphosate, the active ingredient in Roundup. But instead of warning the public, they chose silence.

That case unlocked a new perspective for me. It was one thing to suspect that corporations sometimes put profit ahead of people. It was another to see the receipts—actual documents showing that they knew and still didn't act.

The jury in San Francisco saw it, too. They found Monsanto liable for failing to warn consumers and determined the company had acted with malice. Dewayne was awarded $289 million in damages. It was a landmark moment—not just legally, but emotionally. A reminder that one person's story, when told with courage and backed by truth, can shake the foundations of a giant.

As I watched Bobby take on pharmaceutical giants, I kept thinking back to a TED Talk I'd seen years earlier—*Dare to Disagree* by Dr. Margaret Heffernan. It centered around Dr. Alice Stewart, a British physician and epidemiologist whose story had stuck with me ever since.

In the 1950s, Dr. Stewart uncovered a troubling pattern: children from wealthy families were dying of leukemia at higher rates. She delved deeper into environmental factors and found a common thread: Many of these children's mothers had received abdominal X-rays during pregnancy, something the average person couldn't afford at the time. Her research showed that this exposure was linked to childhood cancer.

When her findings were published, they weren't met with curiosity or concern. They were met with outrage. The medical establishment, doctors, and the nuclear industry all pushed back hard. After all, this flew in the face of everything they believed: that technology was safe, that doctors helped—not harmed—patients. It took twenty-five years before the practice of X-raying pregnant women was finally abandoned in Britain and the US.

The TED talk about Dr. Stewart's discovery wasn't just about medical history, it was about the courage to challenge consensus. I could see my husband in this light. Heffernan spoke about the importance of constructive conflict and the need to surround ourselves with people who think differently, not just people who nod along. She noted our neurobiological urge to seek sameness, and how it can sometimes limit our thinking. Choosing discomfort over familiarity, engaging with people who challenge us—not just validate us—does not come easy.

That idea hit home. I was married to a man who not only believed in constructive conflict, he was leading the charge. I couldn't help noticing that some of the same voices who always supported women's issues seemed less willing to listen to the women, especially the mothers, who were sharing concerns about their children's reactions to vaccines. I didn't have a particular stance on the vaccine issue, but I respected that Bobby listened to those moms when others wouldn't.

I began to see how deeply entrenched people had become in their own camps. The vaccine debate, like so many others, had stopped being about science and started being about identity.

Friend groups were splitting. Families were arguing. The country was polarized.

Somehow, health care—something so personal and so vital—had become political. And Bobby was at the forefront.

Chapter 17

I know several people who grew up admiring the Kennedys from the Camelot days. Some knew everything about the family, but I wasn't one of those people. In our house, we didn't talk about politics. Not once. The Kennedys were never mentioned. I had no real knowledge of them beyond what I learned in my American History classes, which wasn't much.

When I met Bobby, I found it intriguing that he was from a family steeped in American history, but it wasn't his name that attracted me to him. I was already at a place in my life where I had established myself in the entertainment industry. I was used to working with high profile people, so I wasn't drawn in by the family name. My first impression of the Kennedys was that they were genuine, funny, warm and really valued their relationships with each other. I guess this initial impression, one that I carried with me through our years together at The Cape, made what followed so surprising to me.

April 17, 2023, was quickly approaching. This was the date Bobby was slated to make the official announcement that he was running for president. As we prepared for a security detail, we were advised to get our Last Will and Testaments in order. The connotation was sobering.

I knew our lives would never be the same after that announcement. Some of Bobby's siblings warned us that they were not going to support him before he even announced his candidacy. They explained that it would bring unwanted attention to them, which I understood. I empathized with them. So did Bobby, but he strongly felt the need to walk his own path.

At the time, I could see nothing but a mountain of torment ahead. It didn't take long to see that I had miscalculated. It wasn't going to be one long hard climb, a steep slope with a final destination to rest, like Bhutan. It wasn't one solid obstacle as I thought it would be. I soon realized we were standing in front of a swarm of bees, and I was reminded of a story that Bobby and my stepdaughter, Kick, told me years ago.

When she was eight years old, she and Bobby were hiking in British Columbia. It was starting to get dark, and they knew the three-mile trail they had trekked was about to lead them out of the forest and onto a beach. Suddenly, a swarm of bees appeared in their path. Bobby looked at Kick and said, "Sorry honey, but we're going to have to run through these bees."

"No! I don't want to get stung!" she said.

"Look, we have no choice. We can't turn back now, it's starting to get dark, we're almost there," he told her. He looked her in the eye and said, "You can do this. It's going to be okay."

"Dad!" she yelled.

"Here's what you're going to do. Keep your head down, run as fast as you can, and whatever you do, don't scream," he said.

"Why can't I scream? Does it make them mad or something?" she asked.

Unscripted

"I don't know, but you don't want bees flying into your mouth and stinging your tongue," he said. "Now go! As fast as you can," he said as he gently guided her forward.

With her adrenaline racing, she ran as fast as her little legs would take her through the bees with her dad right behind her, making sure she didn't trip and fall.

To this day, Kick says that was the best part of her trip.

"Didn't you get stung?" I asked.

"Oh yeah. A lot. They even burrowed down into our socks and kept stinging over and over again," she said.

"Didn't it hurt?" I asked.

"Of course," she said.

"How could it have been the best part of your trip then?" I asked.

"We did it together. We made it through. We laughed hysterically for the rest of the day. And now we'll always have that memory of the two of us. I'll never forget it," she told me.

The bee story has always stayed with me. I find it to be a perfect metaphor when I'm faced with some of life's obstacles. Sometimes you have to toughen up, keep your head down, run as fast as you can, and try not to scream. It only makes matters worse.

I knew we were about to run into the swarm, each bee waiting to sting. I knew the pain that lay ahead was unavoidable.

The swarm of bees that hovered in front of Bobby and me was made up of news outlets, smear merchants, outraged trolls on social media, political operatives who are paid to start and circulate rumors, infiltrators, spies, leakers, and even some of Bobby's own siblings.

I quickly learned that politics is no place for the soft or sentimental.

Bobby made his announcement in April. It was a great celebration, standing room only, with over a thousand people there. Although he was running as a Democrat, he attracted supporters from all parties: Democrats, Republicans, and Independents. All of our kids were there as well as my family members and various members of Bobby's. My stepson, Bobby III, jumped into Bobby's campaign feet first, while the other kids weren't ready to divert their lives into the public political arena.

Unlike some candidates, Bobby was operating with no upfront war chest, no highly paid campaign consultants, PR firms, and pollsters, but only a skeleton crew of friends, family, and medical freedom and anti-war advocates, almost none of whom had political experience. What his team lacked in numbers and resources, they made up in passion, intelligence, resourcefulness, and enthusiasm. I was surprised at the unusual spiritual component that would show up to drive Bobby's supporters. Many shared his belief that our country needed to unite, regardless of political parties, and they recognized the risks he was taking by putting himself out there.

Some supporters started a weekly prayer circle. I would receive emails letting me know that they were praying for Bobby's safety and the safety of our family. That really meant a lot to me. He had assembled an extraordinarily talented team of people to run his campaign. They had garnered inside intel from the DNC about the key strategies they would use against Bobby: They were going to ignore him, keep him out of the news, pretend he wasn't running, and try to force him to spend his campaign's money on lawsuits they were ready to file against him.

***

Unscripted

As Bobby's presidential campaign was taking off, I was launching a self-care company with Cat. When she was about to graduate from high school, I asked her if she wanted to work together and create a company we could both be proud of—something that would keep us close even while she was off in college. We had been working on it for a year and a half, registering the trademark, creating different skin care products made from natural, organic ingredients, building our website, finding the right aluminum tins for packaging so we wouldn't have single-use plastics in our brand. It was called Hines+Young. Mine and Cat's last names.

Drawing from my cosmetology background and with the help of seasoned professionals, we made natural, eco-friendly products that were great for your skin, and we designed beautiful nontoxic, clean burning candles meant to inspire relaxation.

I could've never predicted when we started working on Hines+Young that our launch would coincide with my husband's decision to run for president. Like most everything that was about to unfold, I did not see that coming.

I took on new responsibilities as an entrepreneur while also navigating the unexpected role of a presidential candidate's spouse. As I was starting down these new paths, many of my LA friends were eager to get back to their lives and careers in the entertainment industry. They were hard pressed to find work during the lock down and were hopeful change was on the way.

***

I was fortunate enough to be a part of an established show, and we were able to shoot our last season of *Curb Your Enthusiasm* as previously scheduled. Our cast was not a particularly sentimental group but once in a while, Jeff, Susie, and I would randomly hug each other and say, *I can't believe this is it*. We were grateful we had twenty-four years together on what turned out to be an iconic show, but we were sad to see it end. That being said, Larry liked to keep things light.

In Season 5, Episode 10, he died for a few minutes after surgery from giving Richard Lewis one of his kidneys. Jeff, Susie, Larry's father, played brilliantly by Shelley Berman, and I stood around his hospital bed. I was holding his hand and talking with him when he took his last breath. After the first take, Larry asked me what I was doing. I told him, "I'm crying. It's just so sad."

"Don't cry. It's not funny. Just go straight to the rabbi and ask about my will. Then you and Jeff will argue about the five thousand dollars he owes me," he said.

"But what about the reality of the scene?" I asked.

"That *is* the reality of the scene. Jeff paid me five thousand dollars less than the Blue Book value of my car. You want that money back."

His guides in Heaven, played hilariously by Dustin Hoffman and Sacha Baron Cohen, decided they didn't want to let him into the Pearly Gates after a squabble about a DVD case and sent his soul back to his body so Larry could resume his life. What could have been the end of *Curb* turned into a great season finale instead.

Many actors from previous seasons were part of our final season, including Jerry Seinfeld. I got to ask him if he remembered being interviewed by me when he performed at the University of Central Florida in the eighties, before *Seinfeld*. He had no recollection of the encounter. I told him it was actually the first time we ever met. I was a student at UCF, and he performed at our homecoming event. I loved him as a stand up and somehow, I arranged to interview him for our newscast. His reps called and tried to cancel because of his tight schedule, but I pleaded, "No, no! You can't cancel. Please. It'll be so fast. Just give me five minutes."

They called back and said he'd do it, but he would have to leave after five minutes. I was elated. Determined to keep my word, I made sure everything was set up and ready to shoot as soon as he sat down. There was only one camera though, so I had to make a tough decision. Did I frame up a two shot to include both Jerry *and* me? Or did I keep the camera on Jerry the whole time? Oh, I wanted that close-up of Jerry, so I kept the camera on him. As expected, he was funny and gracious. When he left, I had to film myself asking the questions and laughing at his answers. There is footage out there somewhere of me, alone in a gymnasium, pretending to ask Jerry questions, looking at an empty chair and saying, "That's so funny, Jerry! Now, what makes *you* laugh?"

***

The very last day of shooting *Curb* was emotional. The final scene of the series took place on a plane, and we were all together; Larry, Jeff, Susie, Richard, JB, and Ted with our exceptionally talented director/producer, Jeff Schaffer, at the helm. When Schaffer declared it was a wrap on the series, Larry tried to leave the set as quickly as he could. He didn't make it out before his longtime friend, Richard Lewis, said, "I just want to say something. Larry David has treated me like a god, and all of you have. This is the greatest experience of my career, and I love each and every one of you. I'm honored to be working with arguably the best sitcom writer in the last two centuries and God bless all of you. And thanks for being so sweet to me."

Richard's touching send-off had captured the sentiment many of us were feeling. Without saying a word, Larry continued off as the rest of us fought back the tears while, after twenty-four years together, we said our goodbyes.

***

Unfortunately, the entertainment industry was grinding to a halt. The WGA, Writers Guild of America, went on strike, which meant no one was allowed to film anything until it was resolved. It was a gut punch to the industry, but it was important for the writers to establish safeguards to their jobs from the use of AI. The community badly needed to get back to work. Everyone was already struggling from Covid, which had shut down production for so long. Writers, teamsters, actors, prop makers, hair stylists, make-up artists, and costume designers were all struggling financially. Nevertheless, they supported the writers.

I was glad I had started Hines+Young because it was outside of the entertainment industry. I wasn't sure what kind of acting opportunities would come my way after *Curb* ended, and I wanted to create something I would love. After all, I was thirty-four years old when I landed Curb and that was twenty-four years ago. It was hard to know what roles would be out there for a woman approaching sixty. Once in a while, a friend would ask me if I felt like I was being iced out of Hollywood because of Bobby's politics and my marriage to him. I'd tell them the truth: I didn't really know because no one was working due to the strike.

***

The level of passion against Bobby, from both friends and strangers, was often jarring. I was always surprised by the number of people who feel the need to express their strong feelings about

Bobby in public venues. I found some of these demonstrations fascinating.

I happened to see a lady jump up from her seat in a restaurant as we were arriving. Abandoning her surprised date at their table, she bolted outside in pursuit of Bobby and me. Poking her face into the open door of our car, she screamed, "Fuck you!"

Bobby turned to me and asked accusingly, "What did you do to that lady?"

Another passionate woman stood for a long diatribe denouncing us in a crowded Palm Beach resort during the height of the dinner hour.

Equally fascinating to me was the reaction of the upscale patrons who ignored her altogether.

It was such odd behavior to me, and whenever this sort of thing occurred, I was always struggling to get out my cell phone to grab a video of the spectacle.

By the winter of 2023, things started to normalize a little. Bobby and I decided to have a small holiday party. It seemed like a good time to bring our friends together because the lockdown was over and some of us were ready to see other human beings face to face again. Although a lot of people still had strong feelings about the vaccination situation, I felt like I could create a space that would feel comfortable for anyone ready to dip their toes in the social pool again.

I asked my assistant to make an invitation. I wanted it to be light and joyful. For peace of mind, we asked people to test negative for Covid before they arrived. We used the honor system. We didn't need to see a negative Covid test from anyone; we assumed our close friends would stay home if they were feeling ill or tested positive. My assistant took it upon herself to add "or be vaccinated."

I didn't push back on it because some of my friends felt safe from Covid if they had been vaccinated. I thought it was fine.

The party turned out great. We had everything—adorable holiday-themed alcoholic and non-alcoholic drinks and twinkle lights in the garden for those who preferred being outside. A fisherman friend of Bobby's shucked oysters at an outdoor oyster bar. I had our guests play a game where everyone picked a marble out of a hat and had to find the person who was holding their matching marble. The first five duos that matched, got a prize. My new assistant passed out the marbles.

"Do I have to ask Oliver Stone to take a marble? He doesn't seem like he'd be up for this," she said.

"Yes!" I said. "Otherwise someone will be left without a match."

"Okay," she said. "Here goes."

I watched her walk up to Oliver and explain the game to him. He reluctantly reached into the hat, took a marble and immediately put it in his pocket. It was clear whoever had Oliver's matching marble was going home empty-handed. Kathy Hilton, however, found her match and went home with a brand-new *Curb Your Enthusiasm* mug.

Unfortunately, I had invited someone who turned out to be an untrustworthy political pundit friend. He must've felt like he hit paydirt. Of all the people we invited, I had known him the least but never thought he would exploit our friendship. He must have leaked a story to the press, anonymously, that Bobby had demanded our party guests be vaccinated before they were allowed into our home, which wasn't the case.

The Hill reported, "Guests of a holiday party thrown at Robert F. Kennedy Jr.'s home were urged to be vaccinated in order to attend, according to a report by *Politico*." It's possible he had strategically only given *Politico* two words from the invitation—be vaccinated. Nothing else from the invitation showed up in the stories that were printed. This is exactly how the invitation read:

JINGLE & MINGLE

YOU'RE INVITED TO A HOLIDAY PARTY AT
CHERYL & BOBBY'S NEW DIGS

FESTIVE ATTIRE &
GOOD ATTITUDE REQUIRED

SATURDAY, DECEMBER 11TH AT 7:00 PM

... There's plenty of outdoor and indoor mingling space. Out of an abundance of caution, please have a negative Covid test or be vaccinated ...

That little pundit must've been beaming with pride as the news outlets covered the Jingle & Mingle faux scandal ad nauseam. For the record, Bobby didn't have a hand in the invitation or the planning of the party, other than picking out the oysters and more importantly, making a Mignonette sauce that went with them. Also, for the record, I've never heard the words mingle, jingle, festive, or digs come out of his mouth. Bobby responded to *Politico* with this statement:

> *Politico* and other news outlets have written near-identical stories regarding a recent holiday party at my home. The angle of these stories is that I required guests to be vaccinated in order to attend. I did not. I believe that every person has the right to make health decisions free from coercion, threats, or

force by governments, employers, and fellow citizens. I don't always agree with the decisions of others, of course, but I always support their liberty to decide for themselves. I extend this respect to everyone including colleagues, friends, and family members.

Alas, the die had been cast. The story of his supposed hypocrisy became another false narrative among the political media agencies throughout his campaign. Even in Bobby's Senate hearings, before he was confirmed as Secretary of HHS, a senator brought up the holiday invitation as part of the arsenal of character assassination. Needless to say, I haven't mingled or jingled with that pundit since.

It was my first foray into politics and the spin that lights people up.

For the rest of the campaign, the media consistently tried to paint Bobby as a hypocrite, a charlatan, and various versions of insane. They seemed determined to find creative ways to get clicks. Bobby was always unperturbed. He has much thicker skin than I do. I despised the constant destructive chatter.

***

Twenty-four-hour security was a new element in our house, and Bobby's campaign hired Gavin de Becker & Associates (GDBA), the best security detail out there. They were well trained, very professional, and for some reason, they were all handsome. Two of our nieces were living with us at the time. Kailey and Kathleen would entertain each other daily by coming up with reasons to go into the garage where they were headquartered to see who was on duty.

I'd find myself having one-sided conversations with the security detail all the time. Sometimes I'd forget that they weren't there to chit chat. I came home from running an errand and had a nice exchange with one of the guys.

"Wow, the traffic is crazy out there," I said.

"Yes ma'am," he said.

"Well, I know you're probably thinking, it's LA, traffic is always bad, but it was even worse today for some reason," I said.

"Yes ma'am," he responded, making little to no eye contact with me as he surveilled the surroundings.

"I probably shouldn't wear these shoes anymore. They're giving me blisters. See that?" I said as I showed him my heel. He glanced at it briefly.

"Yes ma'am," he said.

"I don't know. Maybe I just need to break them in. I wonder if any of the kids are home," I said.

"Yes ma'am. Cat, Kick, Kailey, Finn, and Kathleen are on the premises," he said.

"Oh. Okay, great," I said. "I guess I need to start thinking about dinner. Do you need anything out here?" I asked.

"No ma'am. We're set," he replied.

"All right then. I'll see you later," I said.

"Yes ma'am," he said.

It was nice having someone to talk to.

***

Bobby was on the road campaigning, going from state to state in an effort to meet voters. He and his team were working overtime, holding rallies and town halls. While he was zigzagging across the country, I was with my brother and sister in Florida working on Hines+Young in our warehouse, preparing holiday gift sets. We had created a fun workplace and spent time there when we could. We'd blast AC/DC and even brought Cracklin' in to do final touches on our packages before we sent them out. It was a real family affair. We had chosen to set up in central Florida because it was close to where our products were being manufactured and also because it was close to where my siblings and my mom lived.

One day, we were having a great time when I received a call from my business manager. He said our life insurance company wanted to offer us additional coverage for Kidnapping and Ransom. The new insurance proposal was complete with the amount of money our family would receive if we were kidnapped, killed, and dismembered. If we were just kidnapped and killed, the survivors would get less.

My family was already concerned about our security. The fact that Becky's son, Jackson, now a twenty-one-year-old, was on the road with Bobby working on the campaign as his body man, only heightened our safety concerns, and I didn't want them to hear my end of the conversation. I thought it might be disturbing to hear the kidnapping and dismemberment talk. I stepped outside to take the call.

Bobby and I ultimately decided to just stay with the life insurance policy we currently held but the conversation intensified my worry for his safety. It was hard to get through a week without someone reminding me of the assassinations of Bobby's father and uncle. Journalists and podcasters often questioned Bobby about his concern for his own safety. *"Aren't you afraid of getting shot?"* they'd ask. Even though Bobby wasn't dissuaded by the security risks, not a day went by without it being top of my mind.

Bobby applied for Secret Service protection five times during the campaign. His application, filed by his GDBA team, declared sixty-three proofs of death threats. It was frustrating that the

White House would deny Bobby Secret Service protection. News outlets and social media commentators claimed the reason for the Biden administration's denial was that it was only "legally available" to presidential candidates 120 days before the election. I knew this wasn't exactly true. Bobby's uncle, Senator Edward Kennedy, received Secret Service protection 441 days before a presidential election, even before he had formally announced his candidacy. Barack Obama, then a senator, received Secret Service protection 551 days before the 2012 election. Ben Carson received Secret Service protection in 2015 while he was running in the Republican primary, 369 days before the election. The list goes on and on.

One journalist, Jeremy R. Hammond, wrote a great article titled, "Setting the Record Straight on the Denial of Secret Service Protection to RFK Jr." It was nice to know we weren't the only ones who saw the great disparity.

Bobby was the first presidential candidate in recent history to request protection and be denied. He is the ONLY candidate ever denied since the 1968 law authorizing Secret Service protection for presidential candidates was enacted after his father's assassination during his campaign.

***

For us, the threats were very real, whether or not the media and the Secretary of Homeland Security were willing to acknowledge it. In September, an armed man was arrested at Bobby's campaign event in Los Angeles. He was wearing two shoulder holsters, carrying loaded pistols, and had a backpack with a laser sight pistol, spare ammunition clip, and other weapons. He asked to see Bobby in his green room. He had even posted on social media that he was going on a mission and might not make it back. The man had what appeared to be a US Marshal badge on a lanyard and a belt clip with a federal ID. One of Bobby's GDBA protection noticed that the US Marshal's badge was too shiny and apprehended the man until the LAPD was able to arrest him. He was charged with carrying a loaded firearm, carrying a concealed weapon, and for impersonating an officer. The police seemed unconcerned and almost immediately set him free. Still, no Secret Service protection.

I was sick with worry about Bobby's safety. I kept hoping that the Biden administration would reconsider granting Secret Service protection. This latest attack was carried out in a public place and was well publicized. It was more than hate mail or threatening texts.

Every day seemed to bring a new security concern. Our house sometimes felt under attack. One intruder made it to the second floor of our home before we got private security. The next month, I was at home on an Instagram Live stream with a high school friend named Lise. We were talking about baking, being moms, Hines+Young, and the benefits of those damned relaxing candles.

Sitting at my desk that overlooks the backyard, I looked up and saw an intruder coming toward the house, carrying something I couldn't quite make out. He clearly wasn't anyone I knew and looked rather unhinged. I was distracted and alarmed but wasn't sure what to do at that moment. Lise asked me a question, but I wasn't listening. I was thinking, *Do I give this a beat and see what happens? Do I tell this live audience what's happening?* Lise noticed my hesitation and asked if I was okay.

"Um, I might need to wrap it up here," I said, as I watched our private security detail, weapon drawn, apprehend the man.

It was only 10:00 in the morning as I watched security handcuff the unhinged man. My day can only get better, I thought. The LAPD showed up, and he was quickly arrested.

Unscripted

Around 5:00 p.m. the same day, after being released, the intruder returned and was arrested again. The story was made public. The next day, I went on podcasts with Bobby to recount the event and talk about the need for Secret Service protection.

Bobby was continually vocal about his Secret Service requests, but to no avail. The media sided with the White House, mocking him for asking.

I felt sure Bobby's siblings had to be concerned as well. It's a very resourceful family. Some of them were even working in the administration, so I felt confident that change was coming soon. But that was not the case.

I kept thinking I just needed to make it through the primaries, and by March or April some of the stress would ease. How could I know that my optimism was so misguided?

Bobby's campaign had gotten word from a reliable source that the DNC was cancelling some primaries and awarding their delegates to Biden, assuring Bobby would have no path to a victory. It would not only affect Bobby but also Dean Phillips and Marianne Williamson, who were running as well. His only path forward, he was told, would be to move away from the Democratic Party.

After a great deal of consideration, he decided to switch parties and run as an Independent. He would need to gather signatures in every state, all with different deadlines and requirements. His path to getting on the ballot was a long shot, but it would be quite the uphill battle because the rules to qualify as an Independent are extremely complicated and complex—by design.

"Okay, so how long are we in it before we know if Bobby has a path to victory as an Independent?" I asked Dennis Kucinich, who was Bobby's campaign manager at the time.

"Oh, he goes all the way to November 5th," Dennis said enthusiastically.

"That's over a year from now," I said, as if nobody else in the room had done the math.

I didn't know if I could handle this for fourteen more months. I found half of a Lorazepam in my nightstand that had expired two years earlier. I took it and waited for it to kick in. It never did.

**

As the election dragged on, it was known that political operatives were doing everything they could to keep Bobby off the ballot. It was rumored that Secret Service was intentionally denied so his campaign would have to spend much of their money on his private security. They also weren't shy about going on news outlets to say so: "We view Robert F. Kennedy Jr. on the ballot as a threat to stopping President Biden winning re-election," Matt Corridoni, a spokesperson for the Democratic National Committee, was quoted saying in a CNN article. It seemed never-ending.

Another plan was to drain money by burying him in lawsuits. CBS News reported, "As independent presidential candidate Robert F. Kennedy Jr. ramps up efforts to secure ballot access in all 50 states, he faces stiff resistance from Democratic political opponents attempting to block his November election bid with multiple lawsuits."

Here was the party I had been a member of most of my life, and that Bobby had been a member of his entire life. And now, DNC leaders were bragging about their strategy: Make sure Americans didn't have an opportunity to vote for the candidate of their choice. I switched my political party from Democrat to Independent. I also started switching the news channels around to see how each of them were covering the stories.

Chapter 18

I kept a journal during Bobby's campaign. Before he announced, I had written about how I felt badly for his siblings. Some of them didn't want him to run, even though four of the six had pursued their own political ambitions. Bobby had supported each of them.

On March 17, 2024, the floodgates opened on family matters when, in what appeared to be a strategic move, President Biden posted a picture on social media of some fifty Kennedy and Shriver family members posing with him on the steps of the White House. He had invited them to a St. Patrick's Day celebration, but everyone sold the story as a family endorsement. A handful of Bobby's siblings reposted the photo, praising President Biden, while most opted not to repost it or to comment. The image of President Biden surrounded by Bobby's family got the attention that the Biden camp and some of his siblings clearly intended. I should note that none of our kids were invited to the holiday celebration, not that they would've gone, but the explanation of—*the entire Kennedy family was invited*—would have been a little more plausible. The political spin was getting cranked up and some of Bobby's siblings were doing the cranking.

I had thought that they didn't want to be catapulted into the spotlight of unwanted attention, but on April 18, 2024, Kerry Kennedy took center stage, as Joe, Kathleen, Chris, Max, and Rory stood behind her while the cameras rolled during one of President Biden's rallies. They smiled and cheered as Kerry announced with great gravitas, "That's right, the Kennedy family endorses Joe Biden for president."

Kerry's announcement disregarded the family members who not only supported Bobby, but the ones who were working on his campaign! News outlets obligingly rushed to amplify the bombshell announcement. Kerry enthusiastically leaned into the microphones as she gave her speech.

"When Daddy announced his bid for the presidency in 1968, he talked about the perilous course our country would take under the wrong leadership," she said. ". . . Daddy stood for equal justice, for human rights and freedoms from want and fear . . ."

She quoted her father several times in her seven-minute speech, however, she would later publicly criticize Bobby, again and again, for referencing *her* father during his campaign.

Up until that moment, most news outlets were going out of their way to never mention Bobby was even running. When the siblings took to the airwaves, however, the media couldn't resist. The storyline was, *See? Robert Kennedy Jr. is so bad, even his own family doesn't support him.* The result was ironic, since every time they said his name Bobby would get hundreds of thousands more followers on X, Instagram, and TikTok.

Millions of people tuned in to his interview with Joe Rogan on *The Joe Rogan Experience* podcast to see what Bobby was all about and apparently appreciated what he had to say. His base

Unscripted

grew exponentially. His siblings' condemnation didn't land the way they must have hoped. Many people learned, for the first time, that there was another choice for president, RFK Jr., and were inspired to support his candidacy.

As I watched it all play out on TV, I was flooded with emotions. Of course, I was disappointed and angry, but I also found myself feeling sorry for them for choosing politics over family. I had been so disillusioned by this attack on him. I realized that they were not who I thought they were. Bobby handled the situation gracefully. Despite nearly daily goading by the press to respond in kind, Bobby was disciplined about never responding. Not once during the entire campaign did he breathe a single bad word about his siblings and cousins. I admired him for that.

As Bobby's polling numbers increased, newscasters were struggling to justify his popularity. CNN went so far as to say that it must've been because so many people were confusing him with his late father, Robert Kennedy. That was a stretch. Bobby's father had been assassinated more than fifty years ago. The justification also didn't jibe, considering the majority of Bobby's supporters were young adults who had no memory of, or political affection for, the Kennedys. Yet, they wanted their audience to believe that twenty-five-year-old Americans thought they were supporting someone from a different generation.

* * *

A dominant theme of the Kennedy era had always been the family's loyalty to each other. It was one of the character virtues that had made Americans love them. But Bobby's generation's willingness—even eagerness—to attack their brother so publicly and maliciously initially made me think that maybe I really didn't understand what it was like to be raised in a Kennedy household. After all, Bobby's upbringing couldn't have been more different from mine. Bobby's father was fighting organized crime and advancing civil rights as the attorney general of the United States. My dad was building a stage for me in a strip mall so my theater company could do a run of Neil Simon's *Last of the Red Hot Lovers*.

Bobby's uncle John was the president. My uncle Frank, whose CB handle was "Wheeler Dealer," was hatching get-rich-quick schemes. One of his classics was a plan that would require me to get my toe chopped off by a flimsy shelf at the grocery store. He felt confident he could hit it hard enough to knock it loose, fall on my pinky toe, and slice it off so we could sue the store for all they were worth.

Bobby and his siblings grew up riding horses, traveling the world, and attending the finest schools. My siblings and I grew up swimming in the lake, taking turns looking out for alligators, and went into debt going to state colleges.

Despite all of our differences, the one thing I thought our families had in common was a reverence for family loyalty. I can't imagine a circumstance where I would publicly turn on my siblings or vice versa, especially not over politics. Publicly, Bobby dismissed the criticism, saying that he and his siblings had been encouraged to debate each other at the dinner table starting at a young age. And, I thought, his siblings may have considered their public attacks on him to be an elevated version of those spirited dinner table disputes. I know that some of his family relationships had become strained even before his campaign. Differences with his views on vaccines and the parole of Sirhan Sirhan had created some real resentments and tension. But their public statements about their differences were delivered respectfully and always narrowly tailored to those issues. They never spilled over into the personal attacks that he began to experience the moment he announced his candidacy.

It's true that Bobby's most outspoken siblings would usually end their soap box moments by saying, *"but we love Bobby."* It sure didn't feel that way though. His family members didn't seem content to make the case for President Biden, or, subsequently, Kamala Harris. Their purpose seemed to be to hurt their brother. They used words like "crackpot," "dangerous," "reckless," and "predatory," to describe him, which put not only his life in danger but the rest of our family as well. One of the hardest things to witness was hearing some of Bobby's own siblings claim he didn't share their father's values. It was as if they'd forgotten that RFK Sr. was Bobby's father, too. Bobby's principles were shaped by a lifetime of experience and a deep reverence for his father's legacy. Anyone who has watched Bobby stand up for the voiceless or speak passionately about democracy knows this.

Bobby would encourage me to not let myself be hurt by their words. Yes, it should have been the other way around. I should've been reassuring Bobby, but he seemed able to let the attacks pass over him without disrupting his mood or confidence. The outspoken members of the family grew louder, even reaching the point where his sister referred to their father as "the real Robert Kennedy." That seemed absurd. Bobby *is* Robert Kennedy Jr.—his parents, *their* parents, gave him that name, and he's carried it with his own purpose and conviction.

Regardless, watching his family, who had a reputation for standing by each other through thick and thin, turn on him struck me as sad. Bobby would just keep repeating that they had a right to their own opinion and that he loved them.

***

One sunny morning, like any other day, I woke up, grabbed my phone, and checked my countdown app to see how many more days until November 5th. I foolishly glanced at X to see what was trending. Brain worm? Ok, I'll bite. I clicked to see that it was *Bobby's* brain worm. I was going to need some coffee.

Bobby was on the road at the time, and I didn't feel the need to call him about this one. I remembered, years ago, he told me a doctor had discovered a parasite in his brain. He was informed that it had already died, and there was no further action needed. Apparently, a reporter from the *New York Times* was going through a thirteen-year-old deposition from Bobby's divorce where he had mentioned the brain worm. The thirteen-year-old story caught fire among the mainstream media.

The news outlets were having a field day. At first, they were saying, "He's crazy—he says he had a brain worm." And then, as doctors were interviewed about it, they admitted that it's not that uncommon for people who may have traveled to international jungles or who may have eaten undercooked meat to be found with a parasite. Bobby checked both of those boxes. When we travel, one of his favorite things to eat is whatever a local is selling on the side of the road, out of their truck.

"Well, how much of his brain did it eat?" a newscaster asked with a straight face as he looked right into the camera.

Another reporter was calling for Bobby to release his medical records despite Biden, age eighty-one, and Trump, age seventy-seven, refusing to release theirs. People were really working themselves into a frenzy about Bobby's brain worm. I will admit, that story was one of the most entertaining, and there would be plenty more to come. Bobby made me laugh the most that day though. His response on X really got me.

"I offer to eat 5 more brain worms and still beat President Trump and President Biden in a debate. I feel confident in the result even with a six-worm handicap."

Before I knew it, I realized I had wasted my whole day following the unfolding of the brain worm scandal. Well played, cable news. Well played.

I decided to implement a few new rules for myself. No more looking at X before getting out of bed. Maybe I could even try going entire days without it, and no more watching the news all day—even if I was flipping around to see different perspectives. It was time to shut it down and stay focused and positive.

The brain worm story was only the first of many "microscandals." They seemed like shiny diversions while President Biden was barely seen in public and President Trump was fighting his court cases. Bobby and his team embraced every attack as an opportunity. This gave him a resilience and calmness that carried us through his campaign.

Bobby was good at using humor to diffuse contrived scandals.

When TMZ aired a surreptitiously filmed video of Bobby walking barefoot on a plane, they also aired the video Bobby made as a tongue-in-cheek apology for his conduct. As he delivered his earnest apology, the video panned out to reveal Bobby sitting barefoot in a crowded airport.

One of Bobby's formerly closest cousins anonymously gave a hostile writer at *Vanity Fair* a picture of Bobby eating a goat during a wilderness kayak trip in Patagonia and told the writer that Bobby was eating a dog. After the story was published, in response to the outcry of the dog-loving public, Bobby posted a video of himself cooking dinner for our dogs, Tilly, Ronan, and Litty, as he explained to them that he had never eaten a dog. "It was a goat!"

Each one of these responses went viral on social media, generating millions of views, thousands of new donors, and hundreds of comical memes.

With every new "scandal," the crowds at his events grew.

***

As the month progressed and the brain worm chatter quieted down, it was business as usual. I was hard at work at Hines+Young when I got a call from Becky. She said our nephew, Michael, had choked at school. The school called and told her to come right away. Becky was having a hard time telling me what had happened.

"Is he okay?" I asked.

"They're taking him to the hospital, but it's almost like the principal was telling me he died . . . without saying it," she said quietly.

All they told her was that he choked, had no pulse, but the EMTs got a heartbeat back after he had been "down" for more than ten minutes.

I took the next flight to Orlando and met up with my niece, Zoe, and my nephew, Jackson, who had also flown in. We drove for about an hour and a half to a regional hospital. Becky had warned us to brace ourselves before we walked into Michael's room. She told me that he was very still, hadn't opened his eyes, and was hooked up to a lot of equipment.

She was right. It was devastating to see him like that. Michael was always joyful and smiling, with sparkly light green eyes that lit up a room. His little body was usually in constant motion due to cerebral palsy but, there he was, with his head barely propped up, showing no sign of life.

Unscripted

There was something else happening that I wasn't expecting, though. I had an overwhelming feeling that my late brother, Chris, Michael's dad, was there with us. His energy was all around. It felt like, when you walk into a party and without seeing them yet, you know your favorite person is already there. In that devastatingly sad moment, I found comfort from the feeling that Chris was with us. With Michael. His presence remained while we were there, but I didn't feel it again as intensely as I did when I first stepped into the room.

It was clear to me right away that Michael was gone. Maybe it seemed more obvious to me because I hadn't been there all day with him like they had. Debbie, our dear family friend who had cared for Michael since losing his dad, kept trying to get him to open his eyes. They all were. Becky, Debbie, and Missy had been in that room with him for at least twelve hours straight, hoping to see a flash of his green eyes. I insisted they take a little break while Zoe, Jackson, and I kept Michael company. Jackson played one country song after another on his phone and sang to him while Zoe held his hand and kissed his forehead every few minutes. The rest of our family was texting, trying to get clarification about what was happening so they could make travel plans if needed.

Bobby didn't wait. He heard the news, cancelled his campaign obligations, and was en route. I prayed for strength to help us through whatever was coming next. Michael's condition was unclear. It was hard to know what was going on. Missy and I went to search for someone who could give us any information. We cornered a doctor who was making the rounds in the wee hours of the night.

"We're trying to understand what's going on with Michael. Would you say he's in a coma?" she asked.

He seemed caught off guard by the question.

"I wouldn't say that, no. I'm sorry," and quietly walked away.

Missy and I looked at each other and just knew—Michael wasn't with us. Perhaps he wasn't clinically dead, but he wasn't alive either.

One day turned into two. We were in a small-town hospital, and we needed clarity about how to move forward. Becky, Griffin, April, Mike, and I huddled together for a difficult conversation about how and when we would let him go. Even though Michael was twenty, he had the body and spirit of a much younger kid. He loved Spider Man and Disney World, but he loved nothing more than being with his family. During our annual talent nights, a few of us would be his backup singers. He'd laugh through the entire song as he held his microphone, chiming in on various words. Becky would take him everywhere, shrugging off the physical difficulties of getting him in and out of his wheelchair. I couldn't do it by myself, but Becky could. He had a special love for her. He felt like she understood him.

One time we took all of the kids to swim with the manatees in Crystal River and Becky was determined to get Michael in that water. It was beyond challenging because it required life vests, floating devices, and snorkeling gear that barely fit his tiny body. While it took Becky thirty minutes to get him ready, he was probably in the water for all of thirty seconds. He loved that thirty minutes with Becky more than he liked the thirty seconds with the manatee. I'd say, "Your Aunt Becky is crazy," and he'd say, "I know," as he laughed and hugged her tightly.

The decision of whether or not to take Michael off life support, to literally end his life, felt impossible. If we chose not to take him off life support, he could be kept alive for an indeterminate amount of time, lying still, in a depressing hospital room. The answer seemed evident to me, but Becky believed there had to be something more for Michael. She made the case to try to transfer him to a bigger hospital in Orlando where they might have access to newer technologies or other doctors who were more knowledgeable about cerebral palsy. She couldn't let his life end in that little depressing hospital room. We all held hands and my sister-in-law asked Bobby to lead us in prayer.

Becky began making calls trying to find someone who might be able to help orchestrate a transfer. Against all odds, our friend Ilene found a hospital that would take him. A plan was in motion, but nothing would happen until the following day.

On the second night, April and I were alone in the hospital room with Michael. We'd been talking all night about him and Chris. It was probably around 3:00 in the morning.

"I really feel Chris here with us and I know he and Michael are going to be together," I told her.

"If I knew that for sure, I'd feel better, but I don't know that. I just can't let him go," she said.

I spent hours trying to convince her that somehow, I just knew, but she wanted proof. Well, I couldn't give her proof. And then, out of nowhere, there was a flash of light in the corner of the room by Michael's bed. Like a lightning bolt illuminating the whole space. April and I looked at each other, stunned. It wasn't raining. There was no storm, no thunder. We both saw it, though. I even got up to see if any of Michael's monitors had shorted out but there was no sign of damage.

"Okay, Chris!" she said. "I believe you, Cher. Okay, I believe you."

And, with that, she was able to find a little peace. It's hard trying to explain what happened, but in the following week, I would hear more instances like this one from nurses and doctors. Little inexplicable moments that flash by at a time that seems meaningful to people bidding farewell to a loved one.

The next day, Michael was transported to a leading hospital in Orlando with nationally recognized specialists. They assembled an impressive team of health professionals who monitored his brain activity for twenty-four hours to make an assessment. The news was dismal. As we feared, nothing could be done. Unlike the small rural hospital where this journey with Michael started, however, the Orlando team offered an opportunity that changed everything. They asked: *Would Michael want to be an organ donor?*

Our response was immediate. Now there was a tiny space in our grief for hope for another family. We began meeting with the Organ Donor team. I don't know if any of us have cried harder than when, after days of testing, they told us Michael's organs were viable, and he would change the lives of many people.

The process meant he would stay on the ventilator to preserve his organs. They began checking for matches. Everything had to be coordinated perfectly. It took several days. We were all just . . . there with him. In the hospital. Waiting. My brother Mike and I took the night shifts. Debbie, Becky, Missy, and Griffin took the day shifts. The staff was more than kind as they looked the other way when we'd fill Michael's room with his cousins and friends, play music and sing to him. We have a big family and oftentimes we were all there together. We never left his side.

There were also legal requirements—two or maybe three specific doctors had to be in the room when they pronounced him legally dead. That day came and even through the overwhelming sadness, there was a rare, strange beauty as we all shared that experience together while his brother Griffin held him in his arms for his last rites.

Unscripted

After five days, the doctors were ready for him. We were told the hospital honors a donor with a ceremony they call the Honor Walk when an organ donor is taken to the operating room. Those of us who treasured him most prepared for the somber procession in the waiting room as we listened to *Calling All Angels* and *Amazing Grace* while deep in our own prayers and thoughts.

The time had come. The hospital staff lined the hallways to pay respect to Michael. With all of us walking by his side, Michael was wheeled to the operating room down hallway after hallway, each lined with doctors, nurses, cleaning staff, and administrators. They were all there to pay tribute to Michael and the grave, genuine gift of giving his own life to save others' lives. They silently nodded to us as we went by as a show of compassion for our family. The gesture was beyond moving. It's something I'll never forget.

Michael saved seven lives. The organ he donated that was the most complicated to find a match for, that would most immediately save the life of the recipient, was his heart. My brother Mike sobbed uncontrollably when we learned that his namesake's heart would save the life of a nine-year-old boy.

There are beautiful souls out there alive today because of Michael. He was a hero to us, and to the organ recipients and their families.

His liver saved the life of a forty-year-old mom of a disabled son. She knew nothing of Michael's disability. She told us in a moving note of thanks that she now felt confident she could care for her son through adulthood.

Later that week, we had a service for Michael. Bobby and I picked up my mom from her retirement community with Bobby's GDBA detail. It wasn't every day you'd see a line of black cars with flashing lights pull up in front of her retirement community.

I always loved it when I'd hear one of the security detail say, "I've got Cracklin'."

The ceremony took place outside at a beautiful lakefront estate and chapel. Many of us were able to hide our tears behind the lenses of our sunglasses. The overflowing crowd of teachers, cousins, and friends who came to pay their respects served as a testament to Michael's impact on everyone he met. Bobby's security team stood watch and listened to family members' heart-wrenching tributes. I could see one of the guys rub his eyes as he adjusted his sunglasses. Our security team had spent time with Michael at the UCP gala and when Bobby and I had taken him to Gatorland a few months earlier. Michael was easy to fall in love with. It was hard to imagine that he was gone.

So started the first year of life without Michael, the first summer, Thanksgiving, and Christmas talent show without him. I thought, maybe everything should just be cancelled until we have had time to process what had happened. But, of course, life doesn't wait. I was soon packing up the six articles of clothing I'd been wearing for the last eleven days and was on a plane back to the land of brain worms and online trolls.

The loss of Michael put everything into perspective. It forced me to unplug from the rest of the world for a few weeks and focus on what really matters to me—family. Who you love and how you love them. All the rest is inconsequential. Criticism, bad headlines, good headlines, politics, acting jobs or no acting jobs, strangers' opinions, journalists' motivations, sanctimonious in-laws, and public take-downs would carry little to no weight as I moved through the next chapters of my life.

Chapter 19

Back in LA, things just kept getting more and more absurd. My best friend Rachael Harris lived down the street from us. I first performed with Rachael at the Groundlings, and we cheered each other on as we climbed up the career ladder side-by-side. Rachael delivered memorable performances in *The Hangover*, *Night at the Museum*, *Diary of a Wimpy Kid*, and as a regular on the sitcoms *Suits* and *Lucifer*. We moved in next door to each other so that we could spend more time together. Rachael, who was willing to put aside her growing political discomfort, would come over to cheer me up. I was suspicious that my phone was tapped so she and I would talk in code. Even when we were in person, around the kitchen island, we'd speak in a way no one could ever decode. Including us. Sometimes we'd forget the code names we'd made up for people.

"Did you hear about Crazypants?" I asked.

"Uh huh, so weird. And what about Featherweight? That sounded like a lie," Rachael said.

"Yeah. It was, but then when Sisterwives reposted it, people started to believe it," I said.

"Wait. Who's Sisterwives again?" she asked.

I wrote down the name on a piece of paper and slid it over to her.

"Oh, right. I was thinking she was Cotton Candy," Rachael said.

"Should we watch *Dancing with the Stars* to get our minds off of things for a while?" I asked.

"Yeah. I didn't come over to talk about *The Grapes of Wrath* all night," she said.

***

As the first presidential debate crept closer, Bobby's campaign was scrambling to make sure he'd qualify. It was paramount for him to be on the stage with President Biden and President Trump. CNN was hosting it, but because they scheduled it so early, the requirements they set were nearly impossible. Bobby had to submit signatures in every single state just to get on the ballots, but here's the kicker: some states weren't even letting him turn them in yet because their deadlines came *after* the debate. And in places where he *did* submit enough—always hundreds more than required—they stopped verifying them because of lawsuits filed against him.

It was a mess. CNN's rules applied to "presidential nominees," but at that point, neither Biden nor Trump were officially on any ballots, either. Their party conventions hadn't happened yet, so they hadn't been formally nominated. Still, CNN treated them as presumptive nominees, while Bobby was held to a different standard entirely.

Unscripted

Bobby was not in the debate. Calling it a disappointment is an understatement. President Biden's disastrous debate performance had Democrats questioning whether he could win or even serve another term. From that moment on, the momentum shifted in Trump's favor. I would've given anything to have seen Bobby go head-to-head with President Biden and President Trump. I believe it could've changed the course of the election.

Bobby continued his campaign calling for unity in the country. He would speak about the need for bipartisan partnerships. The make-up of his supporters echoed his sentiment. Independents, Republicans, and Democrats continued to show up at his rallies with open hearts and open minds, ready for a change.

A little over two weeks later, on July 13, 2024, I was in Hyannis Port with some of my kids and family. I was in the grocery store trying to figure out what to make for dinner when I got a call from Bobby telling me President Trump had been shot. I was shocked. I was comforted to hear Bobby's voice, though. I asked him if he knew whether President Trump was okay. He said that he had checked on his status and heard he was all right, but the incident had left most people shaken. I was relieved to hear the gunshot wasn't fatal and felt an indescribable sadness for the Trump family.

Clearly, my concern for Bobby's safety during the campaign was for good reason. I wished he wasn't out there in crowds of people every day. The risk was too great. After a few minutes on the phone, I realized I was still standing in the produce aisle holding celery, nearly in tears, as people hurriedly navigated around my shopping cart. It was business as usual for the rest of the shoppers. They hadn't heard the news yet.

As I was making dinner, my mind was racing. Why hadn't Bobby's siblings spoken out about him not getting Secret Service? Many of them were right next door, but unlike previous summers,

I didn't see them. I still had nice relationships with a few, but it felt like a mutual decision to not see those with whom I had once been the closest.

I started thinking back to a conversation I'd had with Bobby when we were dating. I asked him why he thought his Uncle Teddy ran for president after his two brothers were assassinated. Why would he take that risk? Bobby told me Teddy felt a calling to serve his country, regardless of what had happened to his brothers. He pointed out that each of the four brothers had volunteered for military service during wartime even after one of them had died. I can't say that I fully understand it, but I respect it.

Bobby kept calling me in between TV appearances that night. News outlets wanted to talk to him about the assassination attempt. Later, he called me and said President Trump wanted to speak to him. It was almost midnight.

"What? He's just been shot," I said.

"I know. What's going on?" he asked.

"I have no idea, but there must be a reason he wants to connect with you. He's been through a traumatic experience. It seems like you should talk to him, right?" I asked.

"I agree. I wanted to talk to you first," he said.

We both felt politics should be put aside and he should connect with President Trump. I thought it made sense considering the Kennedy family history and the fact that they were both running for president. It made for a lot of unique shared experiences.

Bobby called again after speaking to President Trump at length. Trump wanted to meet with Bobby in person. My anxiety was reaching a new high. What did this mean?

They decided to meet in Milwaukee first thing in the morning on Monday, just before the Republican Convention was to begin.

My therapist was getting desperate texts from me in the middle of the night. It felt like everything was happening too fast.

Many people were outraged by the assassination attempt and quickly started throwing their support behind Trump. Television journalists were reporting that there was little chance for Biden to win considering the circumstances. For the first time, there were serious conversations about pushing Biden out even though he had insisted he wasn't leaving. It seemed inevitable, but who would take his place so late in the game? Word was that it would be Vice President Harris, but how would that happen?

I booked a flight to Milwaukee on Monday morning so I could meet Bobby as soon as he got out of his meeting with President Trump. We would have a chance to talk about everything before any decisions were made, if indeed, political strategies were discussed. When I landed, some of Bobby's security team picked me up from the airport.

"Ma'am, we're taking you straight to the meeting," they said.

"What? The meeting? No, I'm going to see Bobby *after* the meeting," I said.

"Ma'am, Mr. Kennedy is requesting we bring you straight to the meeting. He would like for you to be there."

Oh my God. I wasn't mentally prepared for this and at the same time, I *did* want to know exactly what was being said. I trusted the security detail knew where they were going as we pulled into an underground parking structure. I didn't know where I was, but when they opened the door to the building, I found myself walking through service hallways of a hotel. We were all walking fast, as if I was late. I kept thinking, *I can't be late, I wasn't even supposed to be in this meeting.*

Many more security personnel dressed in dark suits met me and escorted me to a hotel suite. Without hesitating, they opened the door and ushered me in. It was then that I met President Trump for the first time. He had a square white bandage on his ear, reminding me of how close the bullet had come to his forehead. He reached out and shook my hand with a friendly greeting. He commented on my good reputation in the entertainment industry. I replied that he might be speaking too soon. I told him I was glad to see he was okay.

President Trump talked about the shooting incident for a moment, describing how he could hear the bullet whizz by his head. It appeared that his near-death experience had had a significant impact on him. I met Susie Wiles, President Trump's senior advisor and campaign manager. She had a calm, personable yet highly professional demeanor. I gave a hug hello to my daughter-in-law, Amaryllis Fox, who was brilliantly running Bobby's campaign.

Bobby and I locked eyes and gave each other a knowing smile, as if to say, *who knew we'd end up in Milwaukee on a Monday morning talking to President Trump with a bandaged ear*. It was just the five of us. The meeting lasted for about an hour and a half with discussions spanning from politics, to talks about what really mattered in life, to how long someone has to live after being bitten by a black mamba snake. (Apparently, as little as twenty minutes.)

I was taken by the ease and candor with which he and Susie spoke. I mostly listened. At some point, the conversation turned to Secret Service protection for Bobby. President Trump said it was unreasonable Bobby had not been granted protection. At that moment, he dictated a message to Susie and immediately posted it on social media, demanding protection for Bobby. The president talked about the advantages of unifying our two campaigns. Bobby and Amaryllis were interested but non-committal. The meeting ended with President Trump saying he needed to get ready to go announce his VP pick at the convention.

Unscripted

The moment I stepped out of the hotel suite, I broke out into hives. I've never broken out in hives before, not once, but suddenly I had hives all up and down my arms and I could feel them making their way across my abdomen. *Was I allergic to something there?* That night, one of Bobby's staff joked that I must've been allergic to President Trump.

Within twenty minutes of President Trump's tweet, we were informed Bobby was getting Secret Service protection due to a presidential order from President Biden. Bobby had anticipated he'd be granted protection after the assassination attempt, but President Trump's tweet had seemed to provide the impetus. Secret Service reached out to schedule a meeting later that day.

There was much discussion about what Bobby's next move would be. It's fair to say, there were some differences of opinions. It was rather unusual because his team was almost always in agreement about how his campaign should move forward. I had become close with the team through the last year and a half. They were all caring, trusted, smart, compassionate people who had worked tirelessly with Bobby. *Was it time for Bobby to suspend his campaign? And if so, how would Bobby guide his supporters in the election?* We all agreed that his campaign should move full speed ahead while continuing to talk with President Trump and see what would unfold in the following days.

We rushed out for our meeting with the Secret Service. They explained that because their protection had been an Executive Order and had not come from Secretary Mayorkas, the Secretary of the Department of Homeland Security, only Bobby would receive protection. That meant that our immediate family, the kids and I, would not be protected even though this was customary for all other nominees' families. As they talked, I could feel my hives make their way down my legs.

They talked about bomb sweeps that would need to be done at the house with their dogs. We already had three dogs: Tilly, a young bird dog, rambunctious and always looking for a fight; Litty, a sweet female Gordon Setter; and Ronan, a male Gordon Setter who had been a part of the family since I first met Bobby. Fourteen-year-old Ronan was having trouble even standing at times. What was going to happen when they mixed in with the bomb sniffing dogs? The Secret Service informed me that we would need to remove Tilly, Litty, and Ronan during the sweeps. Oh and, also, everyone in the house would need to evacuate during the sweeps.

My hives were going strong. Bobby, the team, and I met for dinner to continue our talks about what the path forward should look like. I could feel something unusual happening with my face. I turned to Stefanie, Bobby's ever buoyant communication director.

"Is there something going on with my lips? They feel strange," I whispered.

She looked at me and quickly replied, "Yeah, your bottom lip is really big right now. You might want to go take a look."

I excused myself to the ladies room, looked in the mirror and could see that my bottom lip had swelled to the size of a baby carrot. Was I still having an allergic reaction to something? (It couldn't have been President Trump, he was on the other side of Milwaukee.) Between my hives and my swollen lip, I was really a sight to see.

When we got back to our hotel room, we began calling doctors for advice. I was taking Benadryl, sitting in Himalayan salt baths, and monitoring the lip swelling. My upper lip started to get involved and my bottom lip was close to splitting in two. I looked like a casualty from *Botched*, the show about plastic surgery gone wrong. Bobby and I decided it would probably be best for me to go home first thing in the morning. In the meantime, Jackson drove me to a walk-in emergency facility. We couldn't stop laughing at my crazy face.

After ruling out an allergic reaction, the doctor asked, "Have you been under more stress than usual lately?"

"You could say that," I said.

"I'd advise you to try to find a way to not be so stressed. Your body is trying to tell you something," he said.

"Oh, okay. I'll work on that," I said as my rubbery lips bounced up and down.

He gave me steroids for the swelling and sent me home with an EpiPen "in case you should have a reaction on the plane and feel your throat starting to close." I flew home with my EpiPen in one hand and hiding my crazy lips with the other. I took note every time I swallowed to see if I could feel my throat closing up or not. It was the perfect kick-off to my new effort in finding a way to be less stressed, as the doctor suggested. This was going to be easy.

Chapter 20

I thought life with Secret Service would be easier somehow, but it made things even more complicated. The new team was nice, but it was a big adjustment. I missed our GDBA security team. My nieces missed our security team too. We knew their names, and they knew our family. There was always a lot going on at our house with the kids, the dogs, and the campaign, but now there was an extra layer of chaos. The Secret Service team was professional but much more rigid.

There were police cars and motorcycles blocking traffic in front of our house. I could hear the honking as annoyed neighbors navigated around them. There were Secret Service agents everywhere, even standing guard by the pool. It was quite a sight seeing Cat and her friends in their bathing suits with a fully dressed man standing two feet away, talking into the device on his wrist. My best friends would have to check in and show ID every time they came over. The dogs would go crazy at the sight of the bomb sniffing dogs.

Unscripted

One morning, I was on my way out the door to go to a much-needed therapy session only to find my car blocked in the driveway by the Secret Service. The person who had the keys was not on the premises. I had to text my therapist and tell him I would be late. I kept thinking back to the sweet Milwaukee doctor who advised me to be less stressed. The more I tried to be "less stressed," the more stressed I got.

***

On July 21, President Biden dropped out of the race and announced Vice President Harris would be running instead. I'd never seen that happen before, but this presidential race had a long list of *never befores*. It was soon after that, a story broke about Bobby and a dead bear. People were outraged, amused, perplexed, or downright angry.

It's not easy understanding Bobby's relationship with animals. He has a love for them like no one I've ever met. He loves the live ones and also finds the dead ones interesting. Why does he bring home dead snakes, turtles, alligators, birds, whale heads, etc, etc? I don't know. Why did my brother wrestle an alligator on the side of the road? I couldn't tell you. Guys are weird. But in all of my years with Bobby, I've never seen him kill an animal. Even when he caught a rattlesnake barehanded in our driveway, he put it in one of my good pillowcases and took it somewhere "deep in the canyon" to release it.

He really does have a way with animals. It's almost as if he speaks their language. One time we parked at the beach, and as we made our way toward the water, we saw people running away. My instinct was to get back in the car and find another spot, but

Bobby picked up his pace to see what was going on. He asked a guy what was happening.

"There's a skunk down there. Everyone's clearing out," he said.

Of course, Bobby immediately beelined toward the skunk.

"Hey, I just got this car. I really don't want to drive home with you after you've been sprayed," I said as he walked away and calmly approached the skunk.

The beachgoers who were heading out stopped to see what the crazy guy was going to do with the skunk. I was also curious. The skunk stopped, turned to Bobby and raised her tail. Everyone gasped. Bobby and the skunk just stared at each other, neither of them moving. After a few minutes, she put her tail down and started walking again. Bobby walked beside her. Every few steps, she'd stop, look at him and raise her tail. When she would decide he wasn't a threat to her she'd lower her tail and start walking again. They just kept walking, side by side, until he gently guided her off the beach into a grassy area away from all of the people.

And it's not just skunks; he seems to be able to communicate with all animals. Early on, I was visiting him in New York. We were in his minivan, driving back to his place in the middle of the night. It was pitch black. Suddenly he slammed on the brakes. "What's going on?" I asked.

"There's a bird in the road," he said.

I hadn't seen it. He got out, picked up the bird, checked all the feathers on one wing, then the other, and said to the bird, "You don't have any broken feathers. You're fine. You can fly." Then he tossed it into the air, and it flew away.

Any given day, when Bobby was at the house, I'd look out the window and see him, shirtless, calling the wild ravens he'd trained to come to him. He'd make a loud *caw, caw* type sound as he threw out bits of meat, then he'd sit still as they came right up to eat out of his hand. Why was he shirtless? I don't know.

When he was on the road campaigning, Bobby would ask my nieces and me to feed the ravens. We would take turns with the birds. Being a vegetarian, I wasn't interested in throwing out meat, but I'd feed them strawberries or bread or something pleasant like that. I couldn't bring myself to *caw, caw*. I'd line the berries up on my bedroom balcony railing and wait until they saw me. I could tell they liked me okay, but I'm sure they were always a little disappointed to see it was just me in my frumpy bathrobe with some old fruit.

***

Politically, tables started to turn. With the newfound energy Vice President Harris was bringing to the race, and the swell of support President Trump was receiving after the shooting incident, it was clear Bobby didn't have a chance in the election. He had millions of supporters, though, who resonated with his platform of improving the health of Americans and finding a way to end chronic disease. If Bobby were to leave the race and endorse one of the candidates, it could move the needle in a very close race. He reached out to both the Harris campaign and the Trump campaign to see if either would be interested in joining forces, so if Bobby *did* drop out, he could continue his work on health issues. The Harris campaign wasn't interested, but President Trump made it clear he shared many of Bobby's goals. Word had gotten out about Bobby's meeting with Trump, and it was causing quite a stir.

Friends started calling me. "You can't let Bobby do this! He's going to get Trump elected! You've got to stop him."

Between the frantic incoming calls and the heart-wrenching cries from Ronan because he was in so much pain, the house was filled with tension. I could've never predicted, not in a thousand years, what was about to happen.

After a great deal of consideration, weighing the pros and cons, it started to come into focus that it was more important for Bobby to continue his leadership in a new health movement by joining forces with President Trump in a bipartisan effort. It was no secret Bobby had been a lifelong Democrat and only recently had become an Independent, but the question on everyone's mind, including mine, was: *Is President Trump being genuine or is he making a strategic move and planning to sweep Bobby aside after the election?* It was a calculated risk, but Bobby had come to trust President Trump. The pros outweighed the cons for Bobby.

On August 23, 2024, Bobby delivered a moving speech to his supporters explaining his decision to suspend his candidacy and throw his support to President Trump. I watched from my living room with some of our kids. It was impossible not to be emotional. I knew how disappointed all his supporters would be. All of the volunteers who had given everything they had for the past year and a half, and all of those who had worked so hard on his campaign, fighting battle after battle—I knew they were all watching. I shared in their disappointment. I had always felt Bobby would have made an amazing president, and even though he was a longshot, I knew if he were in the White House, he would be a great leader. That chapter had come to an end, and another one was beginning. I didn't feel ready. I wanted more time. I was struggling with what lay ahead.

The hours between Bobby's speech and Bobby walking out at one of President Trump's rallies later that night, were dragging on. I continued to field angry calls and texts, which, for the most part, I didn't mind. I was glad that those friends felt connected with me enough to say how they felt. I empathized with them. When Trump was first elected in 2016, I was in a haze. I was unsure of what the following four years would hold, and I was afraid his lack of experience and his boisterous and combative personality would be detrimental to the country. I had only known him from TV appearances and what I'd seen play out during the election.

The morning after the 2016 election, I dropped Cat off at school, then listened to country music and cried for a few hours. I wanted to snap my fingers and move time ahead four years. Then I thought, that would mean I would miss the next four years of her life. That was the last thing I'd ever want to do. It jolted me back into the present.

Regardless of what would play out politically, I had four great years ahead of me with Cat and the rest of my family. I decided not to let politics color the joyful times I had ahead of me. I thought back to the feeling I had during the recount of the Gore versus Bush election in 2000. I detested how it was handled and how it was settled. I had to disconnect from politics, not that I had been extremely involved in the first place, but I had to accept that it was out of my control. The country had moved forward with President Bush. A lot of great things happened in my life during those years. I was cast on *Curb Your Enthusiasm*, nominated for an Emmy, got married to Paul, and had Cat. I can't imagine what those experiences would have been like if I had started and ended every day angered by politics.

***

Besides being the day Bobby would join President Trump onstage to signal to the world he was supporting him, it was also Kyra's birthday. I was staying busy, helping her set up for a party. Despite the political circus, I wanted her to have a good birthday and have a fun night with her friends. Then I got a call from the vet.

"Hello, Ms. Hines, I have Ronan here, and I'd like your permission to put him down," he said.

"What?" I asked. "Ronan is there?"

The phone was passed to a family friend, Gary.

"Hey Cheryl. Bobby asked me to bring Ronan in. He said you two had been talking about it for a long time and you both agreed that it was time to bring him in. He's been in so much pain," he said.

With all that was going on, I guess I didn't even realize Ronan wasn't in the house.

"Well, yes, that's true, I just didn't know it was happening today. Can I speak to the vet again?" I asked.

"Hello Ms. Hines," he said.

"Have you started the procedure yet?" I asked.

"No, we are about to," he said.

"Can you wait until I get there?" I asked.

"Of course," he replied.

As I drove to the animal clinic, I wondered why this was happening now. I knew Bobby had asked his friend to take care of Ronan to save me from the heartache and he must've wanted it to happen while he was out of town. Bobby truly loved Ronan. He couldn't bear the thought of putting him down. I walked in and saw sweet Ronan lying there. He was calm and content.

"Did you already give something?" I asked.

"No, not yet. Take all the time you need. Just let us know when you're ready," the vet said.

"Okay, thank you. And thank you, Gary. I appreciate you doing this, but I've got it from here," I said as we hugged goodbye.

It was the first time I'd seen Ronan when he wasn't shaking. His body was already calm and relaxed. It was almost as if he was telling me he was ready. I'd had the experience of putting a dog down once before. I held Maria's dog for her when the time came because it was too painful for her to do it. Even when you're absolutely sure it's the right thing to do, it's still incredibly difficult.

I lay with Ronan on his blanket for a long time, petting him. It was just the two of us, looking at each other in a quiet little room with the lights turned down. There were no phone calls or news stories or painful cries. It was just two souls sharing a moment of grace.

I went back home and was able to sneak up to my room without anyone in the house spotting me. I was trying to compose myself enough to make an appearance downstairs for Kyra's birthday celebration when my sister called.

"Hey, are you watching Bobby right now?" she asked.

"No, I thought I'd do it in a little while. I don't know if I'm ready. It's been a tough day. I'm worried about how Trump's crowd is going to respond when Bobby walks out. I just don't think I can take it right now," I said.

"Cher, you've got to watch. Trump gave him an amazing introduction and people started chanting *Bobby* when he walked out. He gave a really great speech. I think you're going to be happy," she said.

I watched and just like she said, the crowd was cheering wildly as fireworks sparked in the background. Bobby gave a beautiful speech, he and President Trump shook hands, and another chapter began.

Cheryl Hines

***

Years ago, Larry described me as unflappable in an interview. It seemed like from the moment he said those words, the universe took it as a challenge. *Okay, how about this, then?*

Chapter 21

September 2024 brought a cascade of distressing headlines, articles, and social media posts—mostly about Bobby, but I got in the mix plenty of times. Keeping the pact I made with myself, I was trying to stay off social media as much as I could. When I looked at my phone, I knew something must've happened because I had received a lot of texts saying—*Are you okay? That guy's an asshole*. I was beyond curious to find out who the asshole was.

I had mentally placed some bets on a few names, but Bradley Whitford was not one. Bradley was an actor friend of mine who most famously starred in *West Wing*. I didn't think Bradley was an asshole. I always liked him, and I had a good time with him when I ran into him on a set or at a party. I was quickly directed to his post on X:

"Hey @Cherylhines. Way to stay silent while your lunatic husband throws his support behind the adjudicated rapist who brags about stripping women of their fundamental rights. Gutsy. Great example for the kids. Profile in Courage."

I had so many questions. What kids? Were kids looking to me for political guidance? Were his stand-alone words—"Profile in Courage"—meant to let readers know he knew he had read John F. Kennedy's book, *Profiles in Courage*? The book about senators who showed great courage and stood against their political parties to do what they felt was right even though they would be criticized for it? Was I a senator here? No, that couldn't be it because that would be a compliment of sorts.

Okay, I decided not to read too much into the reference of the book. I guess the words just sounded good when he was drafting his sarcastic message. Why didn't Bradley just call me to see if he could talk me into revolting against my husband, if that was the goal? Or did he think a post would carry more weight? He was successful in getting attention. The post went viral and got a lot of pick-up. Comments were flying left and right, by the Left and Right. It's fair to say, most people didn't like his snarky attack. He opened himself up to a barrage of criticism: *You know you were just an actor on West Wing, right? Who is this guy? Attacking a man's wife because of who her husband is? Get a life and quit cyber bullying. You're exactly what's wrong with this country; sowing division and hate. Who raised you?*

I usually try not to read comments on social media, (I have a friend who describes it as a form of cutting, self-harm) but I couldn't help myself, I was in the mood. I was surprised to see that for every one comment congratulating Whitford on his post, there were thousands and thousands of comments defending me and calling him out as a bully or a misogynist. Most of them didn't mention their political affiliation, but it seemed pretty obvious. That day, reading the comments felt like the opposite of cutting. It was oddly healing.

I was hoping all the activity on X would die down, we'd stop trending, and I would put Bradley's outrage in the rearview mirror, but no such luck. The *Hollywood Reporter*, *Variety*, and *Vanity Fair* ran the story. Even Bill Maher got involved.

"The liberals I grew up respecting, none of them were like this. Going after the wife, even the mafia doesn't do that," he said on his HBO show, *Real Time*. "Well, you know what I think is not gutsy? Mansplaining to a woman—but of course not to her face—how she should sacrifice her marriage, all so you could read something on Twitter that met with your approval."

Although I really didn't want to be a part of this story to begin with and was anxiously awaiting the chatter to die down, I enjoyed Bill's monologue.

***

A few weeks later, I took a break from Hines+Young and went to Italy with my daughters. I was happy to be six thousand miles away from the loud world of the election. I wasn't there for very long, however, before Bobby called to warn me of another breaking story. At first, it was an ambiguous story about a political journalist who said she had some communication with a former reporting subject that had turned personal, also stating that it was never physical. There was a lot of speculation that she was referring to Bobby. The press was running wild with it.

I'm sure I wasn't seeing the full scope of the coverage, but I was seeing most of it. Of course, I hated all of it. The swirl of headlines, rumors, and insinuations was upsetting and overwhelming. I had hit a wall.

My first reaction was a wave of indifference. I didn't care about what had happened, who said what, what was real, what wasn't real, who was involved or why they were involved. I was fine with letting them all continue with the drama and the politics without me. A presidential election is a big business. It seems like the people who put themselves in the middle of it get addicted to all the negative energies. They fan each other's embers until one catches fire. While that fire is burning, someone else is sparking a new flame so there's always something blazing. In this little universe, they can't survive without each other—the press, the candidates, the strategists, the bot programmers, the journalists, the hangers on, the outraged outliers. None of them would survive by themselves. They're all trying to get you to pay attention to them. There's an adrenaline rush that comes with every new story, every new poll. Every day one camp is celebrating while another camp is struggling through a setback. It's done at lightning speed because there's a night when it will all end. Election night, November 5th.

In some ways it reminds me of shooting a film on location. A new world is constructed where everyone who's involved shares the same goal. You're there for one reason and one reason only—to shoot the movie. You work every day, all day and night, capturing the story that a writer wrote, that the director is telling, on film. You're away from your family for long stretches. You miss birthdays and holidays that must've left your kids feeling overlooked or unimportant, but nothing could be further from the truth. They're the most important thing to you. You and your family do the best you can to make it through those few months until you return home again.

It had been about a year and a half since Bobby joined the political frenzy that kept him on the road for the majority of that time. This latest story was leaving me with the feeling of being unimportant to him. It felt like a game people were playing and I wasn't interested in participating. It was the end of the line for me.

Unscripted

I stayed in Europe with my girls for a while. I had little to no privacy for long talks on the phone. Like many mothers do, I decided to table my breakdown until I was alone. I didn't know what was going to happen when I returned home and saw Bobby again, but he was eager to talk to me. He picked me up from the airport and we pulled into a nearby parking lot and asked security if they could give us some privacy. We probably talked for an hour while the security team stood watch over the car. I felt so distant from him. It seemed like the only threads that were connecting me to him were directly tied to all of our kids. I loved each one of them so much. I respected and adored them too much not to listen to what Bobby had to say.

For the next few days, we stopped everything and drilled down on the truth. We locked ourselves in our room and laid it all on the table. We talked about all of the painful times we'd been through in the last few years and what we meant to each other. We analyzed how we had become disconnected and what had kept us together. We went through all of the details about the latest story—what was true and what wasn't. Through those soul-searching days, we tightened our ties that bind.

***

It wasn't long before we were on our separate ways again, but somehow, it seemed like the ground was less shaky. I went to visit my mom for a while. I was banking on the hope that she hadn't taken up reading the *New York Times* or *Politico* and wasn't embroiled in the latest political chatter. Thankfully, I was right, she hadn't.

I thought a relaxing night of Bingo with her at her retirement community would be just what I needed. I was having a great time there with her and her friends but then we happened upon a winning streak that didn't sit well with the others. My mom got Bingo once and I got it twice. I'll admit, it did seem suspicious, but we weren't doing anything other than paying attention to the numbers being called. No matter, the small crowd of seniors weren't happy that we were raking in the prize money. It got to the point that the next time I saw I had Bingo again, I decided to ignore it. I didn't want the wrath of the others.

"Bingo!" the guy next to me yelled out. "She's got Bingo!" Then he turned to me and said, "Look, you don't see it? You've got it right there. B-14 did it for you."

I had to think fast. I could feel angry stares burning holes into the back of my head as I slinked up to claim my $3 prize money. I grabbed the microphone and decided to make an announcement.

"Hi everyone. Thanks for letting me play with you tonight. I don't know how I got on such a lucky streak, but I'd like to donate my winnings back into the prize pool."

Somehow, that really chapped one of the ladies.

"What? Is that allowed?" she yelled out.

The guy running Bingo night grabbed the microphone.

"That's so generous. Thank you. That was going to be our last game, but let's play one more game for this $9 pot," he said cheerfully.

There was a lot of hubbub. I couldn't tell what was happening. Then the irritated lady piped up.

"That was supposed to be the last game. Now we have to stay for another one?" she asked.

Even Bingo was stressful.

***

In the same month, sadly, Bobby's mother, Ethel Kennedy, passed away at the age of ninety-six. We had recently visited her and as always, I had a great time. Even in that late stage of her life, she was still able to make me laugh with her little quips. Early in Bobby's campaign, Bobby and I talked to her about Bobby running for president. She was delighted to hear the news. She told him she was proud of him and asked which of his siblings were working on his campaign. She was in disbelief when he said none and was even more surprised when he told her that some were opposing him. We quickly changed the subject to keep the conversation light. I was grateful to have had that time with her and Bobby.

We flew to Hyannis Port for Ethel's funeral and it was challenging being there for two rather obvious reasons. The first was that it just wasn't the same without her there. Usually, the first thing we'd do when we'd arrive was walk across the lawn to her house and say hello. We couldn't imagine what life would be like there without her. She was the heart of the family.

The second challenge was that we knew we might run into issues being in such close quarters with Bobby's siblings. Besides a family wedding in July, this would be the first time Bobby and his siblings would be gathered, and I was hoping it was going to be healing. Perhaps it would be a chance for them to come together in a time of grief and put politics aside.

As part of a traditional vigil, Ethel was laid to rest in a casket at her house for the days before her funeral. Family members signed up to take shifts, sit with her and pay last respects, to ensure she was never left alone. Bobby and I gladly signed up to stay with her while the rest of the family had dinners together or during overnight shifts. We were mindful of the fact that some family members might not be comfortable being with us for hours at a time and we didn't want to interfere with anyone's grieving process. I was pleased to see that many of our nieces and nephews signed up to be with us during our shifts. They've been such a joyful part of our lives, and we were happy to sit with them as we all told our favorite stories about Ethel.

The funeral service in Hyannis Port was small and private. Bobby had spent the better part of the previous days carefully writing a eulogy for his mother, then came the first disruption. *New York Magazine* would later run a story describing their version of what unfolded at the funeral, citing their source as a "longtime family friend." The article states that his family members "weren't eager to give him the microphone at the service on Cape Cod or the memorial planned for two days later in Washington, DC." This is true. It had previously been decided that Bobby would give the eulogy, but some among the group let it be known that they didn't want to hear from him. He had already written the eulogy and was adamant about honoring his mother. The family agreed to proceed as planned.

We gathered in the small church and the time came for Bobby to deliver his remarks. He is a gifted writer, speaker, and storyteller. His eulogy was a rich and beautiful tribute to his extraordinary mother. The author of the article did admit that "several people sitting in the pews told me they were pleasantly surprised by what they heard. There was no talk of vaccines, no attempt to justify his family betrayal." Of course there wasn't. There was never a chance that was going to happen.

The article went on to say Bobby ". . . had not quite learned when to give up the spotlight, and his speech meandered for so long that eventually the priest felt the need to cut him off." I've tried to restrain myself from delving too deeply into the extended family dynamics during this highly politicized part of our lives, but this struck a nerve. Here's what actually happened, and I'll admit it would have been hard for people in the back to hear what was happening.

The church was riveted listening to Bobby, with a single exception. His older brother began gesturing wildly, cursing, and yelling rude comments from his seat in the front row. Surrounding family members at hand tried to restrain him, and they escorted him out so the rest of us could listen to Bobby. As Bobby continued his moving speech, in an unbelievable moment, the priest approached the pulpit and cut Bobby off mid-sentence.

What is going on? I thought. In what world would a priest disrupt a son eulogizing his mother? He didn't give a nonverbal cue—no nod, no gesture, no eye contact. Not wanting to cause a scene, Bobby gracefully returned to his seat. I've never witnessed such inappropriate behavior in church. It would be an understatement to say I was mad at those two men for their utter lack of respect for Bobby. I couldn't believe it. I was also angry that they behaved that way at Ethel's funeral while we were all there to celebrate her life and mourn her passing.

Many of Bobby's family, including most of his siblings and cousins, came up to him at the reception and pleaded for Bobby to finish his eulogy. The priest even came up and apologized. He claimed he couldn't hear what Bobby was saying, but surmised that he must have been saying something that was upsetting because of his brother's reaction and thought he should intervene. Bobby didn't finish his speech, however he later posted it so anyone who wanted to read it, could. It was a moving, often humorous, elegant tribute to his mother. Bobby remained graceful throughout—never reacting in any way other than with humble modesty.

There was another service for Ethel in Washington DC, at the Cathedral of St. Matthew the Apostle, before she was buried next to her husband, Robert F. Kennedy, in the Arlington National

Cheryl Hines

Cemetery. Many prominent figures were there, including President Biden, former president Bill Clinton, and former president Barack Obama. Each of them spoke eloquently about Ethel.

President Clinton talked about Ethel's faith and how she continued to strive to find wisdom through her experiences. He spoke of her as being the embodiment of love and of the ability to immerse oneself in the wonder that every human life possesses, and went on to say, "she did it naturally, *you think*, but when you get hit as many times by life's blows as she did, it's a discipline. You have to decide whether you will keep your heart open or shut it down. Whether you will still keep reaching out to people or clinch your fist."

I appreciated the idea of choosing to find light in others when you're in your darkest hour as a discipline. That made an impression on me. His words went straight into my heart, as I imagine they did to most of the mourners there.

President Obama also spoke of resisting the pull toward despair.

> We live in a time of such rancor and division and suspicion and loneliness, and we isolate ourselves with gadgets and diversions, and we're encouraged to chase after things that don't last and we have trouble distinguishing what is true from what is false and we succumb to those voices that find it profitable to stoke anger and grievance. And even in resisting such voices we so often find ourselves succumbing to cynicism or despair. What better time then, to remember the life that Ethel Kennedy lived. A woman who understood that our salvation comes from turning towards each other, not turning away. Someone who reminds us by her example, that life

goes on no matter how deep the grief. That there is joy and purpose to be found no matter what hand we've been dealt.

President Biden shared about his overwhelming sense of loss when his first wife and daughter died in a car accident and then again when he lost his son, Beau, to cancer. Ethel had reached out to him and visited him several times during his times of grief. That gesture had an enormous impact on him and helped him find strength at times when he was crippled from heartbreak.

It was good for my soul to hear their different insights about grief. I liked hearing about her accomplishments and stories about when she was younger, but I fell in love with her when she was eighty-three. That was the Ethel I was mourning.

Chapter 22

After all the planning, plotting, cheering and jeering, things finally came to an end on November 5, 2024. In an election that was predicted to be razor close, President Trump won both the electoral vote and the popular vote, making him the 47th president of the United States. He nominated Bobby to be the Secretary of Health and Human Services. Bobby would still need to be confirmed by the Senate in the beginning of the new year though. It was time to brush ourselves off and get ready to run through another swarm of bees.

With the holidays approaching, there was a bit of *All is calm, All is bright* in the air. Bobby and the boys went skiing, while the girls and I decided to stay and have a cozy Christmas in LA, with plans of us all meeting up in the following days. Kyra gleefully volunteered to cook a big turkey dinner for Cat, Kick, Rachael, Debbie, Camille, her brothers, and me. After opening gifts with the girls and having coffee and hot cocoa, I thought we should get that turkey in the oven so it would have time to cook before everyone reconvened later that day. As I came face to face with the giant, raw turkey, I couldn't bring myself to touch it.

"Kyra, I really can't stand to be around raw poultry. I don't have the stomach for it, so maybe you want to rub it down with butter or whatever it is you're going to do to it and stick it in the oven so it'll be ready by this afternoon," I said as Kick and Cat lingered around the kitchen island.

"Cher, I don't really want to touch it either. It's too early for that. Look at it," she said.

We all just stared at the turkey sitting on the counter, still in the plastic bag in which it came.

"I'm going to the gym for a little while," Cat said as she quickly exited the kitchen.

I thought maybe Kick would do it. She's usually good at rolling up her sleeves and getting dirty when she needs to, but for some reason, even Kick wasn't interested in the early turkey rub down.

"Okay, well, a lot of people are going to be here later for a Christmas dinner, so someone needs to get this thing in the oven," I said.

That statement ignited a turkey standoff. No one in our house was willing to touch the damned turkey. I called Debbie. She was coming over later with her kids. I was sure she'd be willing to help.

"I can't get away until this afternoon. Maybe you could send it over to my house in an Uber. I can cook it and bring it when I come," she offered.

"Debs, thank you for that but I'm sure we can figure this out over here. See you guys later," I said.

This was getting ridiculous. I texted Rachael, but she wasn't answering. She was also probably working out. Why hadn't I thought of that earlier? Why wasn't I somewhere working out or at least pretending to, so I wasn't there worrying about the raw turkey? In a desperate move, I texted my ex-husband. Paul lived right down the street, maybe he could swing by and put that friggin' bird in the oven.

Within fifteen minutes, Paul and his lovely pregnant wife, Katherine, were in our kitchen, graciously unwrapping the turkey. I stood there and watched as Katherine, eight months pregnant, without batting an eye, rubbed that turkey down with butter and herbs.

Kyra was happily managing the new workers, telling them when they missed a spot and handing Paul the fresh herbs she had carefully picked for the occasion.

Crisis averted. Who doesn't love Christmas morning with their family?

We ended up having a fun night together, sitting around the dinner table, telling stories and laughing about some of the absurd things that had happened in 2024. Kyra, with her extraordinary sense of style and elegance, had set the table with all of our best dishes, cut flowers from the garden, and had created an atmosphere that made us feel like we were the most important people in the world.

**

As the new year began, things were looking up. The Hollywood strike was finally over, and the industry was trying to get back to work. On January 7, a new challenge hit Los Angeles. Rachael called me.

"Hey, are you watching the news? We have to evacuate. There's a fire in the Palisades," she said as she was picking up her kids from school.

"I know. What's happening? It looked like it was so far away, but they couldn't get it under control," I said as everyone in my house was glued to the TV. "Let me see if I can find a hotel, and we'll meet up later."

Kick, Finn, Cat, Kyra, Kailey, Kathleen, and I packed overnight bags as we called friends to see who might be able to take the dogs for the night. We made plans—some of us would go stay with Conor and his fiancée, Giulia, while some of us went to a hotel. The fire spread quickly. My friends' homes were burning down one by one. Businesses were crumbling. Cat's school was on fire. We were all watching for days as the brave firefighters battled tirelessly against the raging flames.

I've always loved LA and the way the community takes care of each other in times of crisis. The city banded together to help those who had lost everything. Some had lost their homes before they even had time to retrieve their most valuable possessions. Tragically, it was all gone. Truly horrific. From our hotel room, we could see a big, dark cloud of smoke looming over the west side of LA. Sometimes, especially at night, you could see the red line of fire on the mountainside as it was making its way east from Malibu and the Pacific Palisades to Brentwood, the community where we lived. What we expected to be a day or so of evacuations, turned into weeks.

The destruction from the historical fire would, yet again, set the film and television industry back in a way from which it would be hard to recover.

***

Still evacuated, I had to go to DC. Bobby was preparing for his Senate hearings, and I wanted to be there in support. Part of his preparations was something they call "murder boards." I really wanted to see it in action. A committee of seasoned advisors simulated a Senate hearing and grilled Bobby with difficult questions. They threw everything at him. Personal insults, financial inquiries, statistics, rumors, accusations, protester outbursts. I found it fascinating. It was hours and hours of no-holds-barred interrogations. Katie Miller, Bobby's sharp witted transition team strategist, advised me to show little to no emotion as I listened. We were all practicing for what was sure to be a brutal few days ahead.

I took my role very seriously. As I listened to the outrageous questions, I remained unmoved. It reminded me of a scene from a film I had done with Richard Gere. My character had died in a car crash, and I had to act as if I was dead. It wasn't as easy as I thought it would be. Any movement by me would have ruined the take. Richard Gere pulled my lifeless body from the car and dragged me to the riverbank. He held me as he realized the fatality of the crash. I would've given anything to watch Richard in that moment, holding me on the riverbank, but I couldn't—I was dead. As much as I wanted to, I couldn't open my eyes. And if that wasn't hard enough, I could feel ants crawling all over me and had to let them bite me without flinching. Knowing I made it through that, I felt confident I could handle the heat of the Senate hearings.

***

There was a lot of press during the hearings. Even though it had been decided at the murder boards that I wasn't going to sit behind Bobby because it might be distracting, when we walked into the crowded room, Katie overturned the decision and told me to sit directly behind him. He did a good job fielding questions for four hours straight. Of course, that's my opinion and there are plenty of differing views out there. One thing is always guaranteed though, there will never be a time when one hundred percent of the engaged public is going to agree about anything. Even keeping as still as possible, with no notable expression, some late-night talk show hosts thought I was blinking too much or perhaps I was blinking an SOS in Morse code. Just the mere fact that I was there supporting my husband was motivation enough for Laurie David, Larry's ex-wife, to post on social media:

"Cheryl Hines in her best and most watched performance yet as the 'dutiful, adoring wife' setting women back decades."

She really covered a lot of territory with that one. I guess it was a dig at me as an actress, a wife and . . . a women's movement leader? Had I, somehow, set women back to the 2000s or maybe the 1990s? To whatever year she thought I'd set women back, she wasn't happy about it.

Bobby was sworn in as the Secretary of Health and Human Resources by President Trump on February 13, 2025.

***

Regardless of what anyone else thinks, I feel good about putting my family first. I always will. They're the ones who mean the most to me. If I made my life's decisions based on fear of how someone else might feel about my choices, I'd be on a different path altogether. As Rachael always says (and she's not the first to say it), "what other people think of me is none of my business."

With Bobby's new role at HHS, I had to stop sales of our Hines+Young products so there wouldn't be a conflict of interest in the event any of our products ever needed to be approved by the FDA. Even though a lot has changed for me in the last few years, some things are on the same track. I'm producing a new project with my ex-husband, Paul, and we're having a lot of fun with it. At the same time, I find myself traveling to Ecuador with Bobby as a US delegate and going to formal affairs at the White House. One of my favorite events so far was the Governor's Dinner. I sat next to the Governor of New Hampshire, Kelly Ayotte. We were talking about how tough elections can be, and I asked her how she got through hers. She said, "If you know who you are, you get through it."

And I like to think that if you like who you are, you might have a good time doing it.

Chapter 23

Life is like improv—and improv is all about uncertainty. You never know what the scene is going to be. You don't know if it's going to land or completely fall apart. You have to be comfortable in that space of not knowing where the scene is going and resist the urge to control it. Your job is to listen to your improv partner and welcome new ideas. There's no script. You're essentially writing it as you go.

I've always been interested in the idea of happiness and the more I learn about it, the more this idea comes up: The people who are happiest are the ones who are most comfortable with uncertainty. They know to trust, no matter what happens, good or bad, they'll be okay.

My sister once took the *Minnesota Multiphasic Personality Inventory* for a job interview. It's a personality assessment used in mental health and other fields to, basically, see if someone is consistent and truthful, and also to see if there are signs that a person might be dangerous. When the examiner showed her the results, he said she's the only person he'd ever tested with the result of "dangerously optimistic." We still laugh about that.

I loved it though. It's one thing to be optimistic and it's another thing to be *dangerously* optimistic. It means you assume things will always work out favorably, so you're willing to take risks you otherwise wouldn't. I share that same disposition.

"If you could go back and change anything about your life, what would you change?" a friend asked me over dinner. It's a bit of a trick question, isn't it? If you went back and changed one little thing, it would change everything. In that case, I guess I wouldn't change anything. The heartbreaks, mistakes, and disappointments have made me who I am.

I think I've come a long way from when I would bury my school paper if I received anything less than an A. I'm still wondering why I buried them. Why didn't I just rip them up and throw them away? Maybe there was something in me that thought, *When I figure out a way to take this test over, I'll dig up the bad grades and replace them with A's.*

That never happened. Nobody cared if I was perfect but me. I was holding on too tightly. I cried at the *thought* of getting a bad grade when the timer went off and I had to put my pencil down. Even though I still struggle with the concept of time—always wanting to turn it back, freeze it, or fast forward it—I'm getting better at just accepting where I am, in whatever moment time is giving me. Life doesn't let me go back, dig up old tests, and take them over.

And just like my teacher taught me so many years ago, I've learned to save my tears for real loss.

Elisabeth Kübler-Ross wrote in her book *Death: The Final Stage of Growth*, "People are like stained-glass windows. They sparkle and shine when the sun is out, but when the darkness sets in, their true beauty is revealed only if there is a light from within." Rather than focusing on the pain and emptiness of losses in my life, I remind myself to carry the light of those I have loved so deeply.

It's impossible to know what the next chapters of my life will be. I couldn't have predicted any of my previous chapters, so there's no point in speculating about my future. But if *"The very essence of romance is uncertainty,"* at least it's sure to be full of romance.